Beyond the Final Whistle

'A politically-committed love letter to all football fans out there who still care about the sport; and to anyone who cares about our life in common.'
—Giorgos Kallis, ICREA professor, ICTA-UAB

'A delightful exploration of football, capitalism, and the difference between the incessant pursuit of more for its own sake and the possibility of making a meaningful life with others in common.'
—Yochai Benkler, author of *The Wealth of Networks: How Social Production Transforms Markets and Freedom*

'*Beyond the Final Whistle* resonates deeply with my own journey in using football to spark meaningful change. This book is a profound reminder that football is far more than a sport; it's a canvas for building a fairer and more compassionate world. Vasilis weaves these truths into a compelling call to action, showing how each of us can play a role in creating a better future.'
—Kelly Davies, Retired International Wales Football Player and Co-Leader 'Sport for Changemaking' Global Team

'This tremendous book encourages readers to see the politics in the cooperation that makes a match possible, even if it is often shadowed by the spectres of big business. This is an incitement to take back the game, and begin to make it beautiful again.'
—Martin Parker, Professor of Organisation Studies, Bristol University

'If you love football and sharing, Kostakis takes you on a deeply personal tour, explaining how the two can be a pair rather than opposites, brilliantly arguing for football less as symbol than as symptom of what has gone wrong in our structured living-together – and how it could be (made) better.'
—Wolfgang Drechsler, Honorary Professor at the UCL Institute for Innovation for Public Purpose

'In a world where culture faces serious manipulation by populist and authoritarian leaders, Vasilis Kostakis presents an inspiring narrative on how culture and sports can become levers to promote democracy. A compelling read for all; football fans or otherwise.'
—Maria Kaika, Professor of Urban Regional and Environmental Planning, University of Amsterdam

Beyond the Final Whistle

Football for a Better World

Vasilis Kostakis

First published 2025 by Pluto Press
New Wing, Somerset House, Strand, London WC2R 1LA
and Pluto Press, Inc.
1930 Village Center Circle, 3-834, Las Vegas, NV 89134

www.plutobooks.com

Copyright © Vasilis Kostakis 2025

The right of Vasilis Kostakis to be identified as the author of this work has been asserted in accordance with the Copyright, Designs and Patents Act 1988.

British Library Cataloguing in Publication Data
A catalogue record for this book is available from the British Library

ISBN 978 0 7453 5073 8 Paperback
ISBN 978 0 7453 5075 2 PDF
ISBN 978 0 7453 5074 5 EPUB

This book is printed on paper suitable for recycling and made from fully managed and sustained forest sources. Logging, pulping and manufacturing processes are expected to conform to the environmental standards of the country of origin.

Typeset by Stanford DTP Services, Northampton, England

Simultaneously printed in the United Kingdom and United States of America

EU GPSR Authorised Representative
LOGOS EUROPE, 9 rue Nicolas Poussin, 17000, LA ROCHELLE, France
Email: Contact@logoseurope.eu

Contents

How this book was written — viii
Funding acknowledgement — xi

Introduction — 1

PART I: WHAT IS FOOTBALL?

1. Football is art — 7
'The tragedy of defeat rendered our struggle indelible' — 7

2. The football gods are dead — 11
'Poets don't know what they're saying' — 11

3. We always dance together — 14
'*Mitakuye Oyasin*' — 14

4. We always sing together — 20
'Well-a, whosoever told it, He told a dirty lie, babe' — 21

5. It came home — 24
'Women are emotional, that's why they concede more goals' — 24

6. So what is football anyway? — 27

PART II: WHAT WORLD DO WE WANT?

7. We all kicked a ball once — 31
'Mystery is the source of all true art' — 32

8. The one who always kicked the can	34
'Life is absurd! Let's play some ball'	35
9. The hallowed lost penalty	37
'How can the world remain silent in the face of something like this?'	38
10. Messi stretches to infinity	41
'Come, the Amazon belongs to you'	41
11. The tragedy of our times	44
'It is difficult to understand something when your salary depends on you not understanding it'	44
12. When you're 4–0 down in the 89th minute, can you turn the tide?	47
'A climate Qatar-strophe unfolds before our very eyes'	47
13. The poor are poor because they make poor choices	52
'You've made your bed'	52
14. The tunnel to the other side of the earth	56
'We are sorry for the inconvenience, but this is a revolution'	58
15. The Cruyff turn	63
'Could you patent the sun?'	64
16. So can the world change through football?	67

PART III: HOW TO CHANGE THE WORLD THROUGH FOOTBALL

17. The turn of the century	73
'I don't think I should stand up'	73

CONTENTS

18. Drivers should drive and footballers should kick the ball — 76
'I can't live on an island that is encircled by poverty' — 76

19. Democracy in football, democracy in society — 79
'Win or lose, but always with democracy' — 79

20. Perhaps the greatest match of all time — 85
'Things are more complicated' — 87

21. Another world is here — 92
'Why the commons need not be another pipe dream' — 94

22. The football of change — 102
'This was the experience of a lifetime but it won't be the last' — 104

23. So how do we change the world through football — 113
¡*Ya basta*! — 114

Sources and further reading — 117
Index — 128

How this book was written

This is a book written for togetherness and it was a communal effort. I'm the main author, but the book wouldn't exist without community.

I started writing it three days before surgery for my torn ACL in 2022 and finished it when I started walking crutch-free again. Of all the articles and books I've written so far, this book represents who I am the most. Just because it was written in almost 30 days doesn't mean it is a sloppy piece of work. On the contrary, it's the most real thing I've ever written. Its lines have existed within me for many years; its lines have had many authors.

Let's start from the beginning – the 1990s, when I first played football. The first authors of the book were my friends in the neighbourhood I grew up in. In the Lakkomata neighbourhood of Ioannina. We played football on a bumpy field that ended in a small concrete cliff. The cliff no longer exists and the ground has been mercifully flattened out. I feel hints of the pure excitement I shared playing with those old friends every time I pass through my old neighbourhood. Thank you wherever you are.

Moving on, some lines were written by my teammates and opponents on the few artificial turf pitches of Ioannina more than 20 years ago. The coaches and kit managers. But especially the latter. They were not getting paid. And yet they collected the jerseys, shorts, and the always dirty socks we threw on the floor after wins, losses, and draws. They were the first to show me so clearly that people don't always do things for money. Thank you wherever you are.

Many lines, perhaps most, were written with my brother. Five years younger but infinitely more gifted than me at football. We played together. Uphill, downhill, artificial, and dry. From the age of 10, he'd been dazzling 15-year-olds. So much so that some of them would rather fall off the little concrete cliff to find peace. People went to the pitch to watch him play. Once, a coach from Ajax was one of them. The two of us moved to the Netherlands. He was 15, I was 20. I dropped my life in Greece for my brother's football dream. He went through adolescence with me.

I saw him fall and pick himself up – repeatedly – literally and figuratively. Until one day he fell, had surgery, got up, fell again, had surgery again, and, at 20-something, that was it. My brother and I experienced first-hand all the dirt and stench of professional football. I stopped watching football. I went into a self-imposed exile. Until I became a father. My son started playing and watching football no matter how much I tried to prevent it. At the same time, my brother returned to amateur football for our village's team. And so, I too returned from exile.

Lines were written by my friends, fellow students, and teammates in the university team in Thessaloniki. I don't remember any goals, not even the cup. I remember the pleasure of losing and winning together. I left for the Netherlands and abruptly ended our moments together. The fact that they ended like that made them unimaginably precious. Thank you (I know where you are).

Many lines, the most politically loaded ones, were written with friends, colleagues and collaborators in the universities and research institutions where I work as well as in our research collective, the P2P Lab. Other lines were written on Tuesday mornings, in conversation, in front of a fireplace during winter and on a big wooden swing during summer, at the Thimomeno Portraito (Angry Portrait) in Ioannina. Thank you (I know where you are and where you live!).

My heartfelt thanks go out to all the wonderful people of Pluto Press. Special gratitude to Jonila Krasniqi, who initially introduced me to David Castle. It was David who ultimately decided to take the risk and move forward with the draft of this book. I am also deeply appreciative of the anonymous reviewers who shouldered the task of reviewing early drafts of the book and offered invaluable feedback.

Also, thanks to Nikiforos Tsiours and Chris Papageorgiou. They were the first readers and the ones who saw the book grow daily. Their comments and support pushed me to start and finish it. With them and several other friends, we established the AnotherFootball Foundation to bring the ideas and vision of this book to life, both on and off the pitch.

Thanks to Yorgos Konstantinou (aka yorgos) for the illustrations, which are used under a CC BY-NC-SA 4.0 license (https://creativecommons.org/licenses/by-nc-sa/4.0/).

Last, my deepest thanks to my family (including Chris Giotitsas). For everything.

Funding acknowledgement

One of the motivations behind writing this book was to communicate to a broader audience the gist of a five-year-long research project named 'cosmolocalism'. Cosmolocalism, funded by the European Research Council and coordinated by myself, explored real-life transitions to post-capitalist futures. Hence, I acknowledge funding from the European Research Council under the European Union's Horizon 2020 research and innovation programme (Grant Agreement No 802512). More info on the project can be found at cosmolocalism.eu.

However, they won't say: the times were dark
Rather: why were their poets silent?

> – Bertolt Brecht (1898–1956)

Delete Facebook and let's play football in the rain.

> – Writing on a wall

Introduction

This book presents a novel perspective on football by exploring its potential as a catalyst for social change. Rather than focusing on the practicalities of playing the game or revisiting its history, I look forward and ask: Where do we go from here? How can we address the current state of football and, by extension, our world?

Today, football faces numerous challenges. Corruption plagues its highest levels of governance, with bribery scandals and financial mismanagement tarnishing its reputation. Excessive commercialisation has led to astronomical player transfer fees and wages, and rising ticket prices, alienating many fans and smaller clubs. Corporate interests often overshadow the sport's communal spirit, threatening its integrity and accessibility.

While acknowledging the value of historical accounts and the rich field of football studies, this work takes a different approach. It uses football as a lens to explore and imagine a post-capitalist future. My goal is to nurture a shared vision of an alternative path forward for the sport, with implications that extend far beyond the pitch. At its core, this book pursues a post-capitalist political economy, one we can prefigure through football. By examining the sport critically, I try to demonstrate ways to envision, experience, and construct political and economic frameworks that significantly improve upon our current systems.

This is not a scholarly contribution to the field of football studies, but rather an invitation to reimagine the sport's role in society. Through football, I aim to inspire readers to consider new possibilities for social organisation, economic structures, and community-building. In doing so, I hope to spark conversations and actions that could lead to meaningful change both within and beyond the world of football.

My day job is that of a University Professor. I teach, research, and write articles and books that few people read, and fewer still will understand. Not because I have a great mind. Sometimes even I struggle with what exactly I wish to communicate. And I am not alone in this. The complexity of academic work often makes simplifying concepts for accessibility a deeply challenging task.

Here is my attempt to broadly describe what I do: My work is about how people create things: software, wind turbines, prosthetic hands, farm machinery, paintings, music, and more. Sometimes people produce things, and that act makes them happy. Other times, people find no meaning in their work. Sometimes they create beautiful things. Sometimes they create things they are not proud of but have no choice. Sometimes they do it for the money alone. Sometimes they do it because they find joy in creation. Occasionally they do it for both these reasons. Through my research, I strive to explore ways to produce so that as many people as possible can have happier, more sustainable lives.

This book, then, is about social change. It is an attempt to establish a frame of reference, or a common vocabulary, guiding my struggles to translate the above-described work into something concrete and lived for a large number of people. It begins with questions that may seem purely football-related, but they are much more than that: What does it take to score a goal? Who contributes to that? Why does credit typically go to top scorers alone? Why do some athletes make millions while teachers and scientists do not? Why do we play and/or watch football?

It ends with questions like: How does football affect global inequalities and the climate crisis? How will our children learn through football that the game itself, not winning, is what matters most; that in school, it is knowledge, not top grades, that is most important; and that in adulthood, it is genuine connections with fellow human beings and nature, not money, that brings the most fulfilment?

The book is split into three parts. Each part is accompanied by references to the sources upon which I relied, along with recommendations for further reading. In Part I, I explain what I understand of the concept and lived reality of football. I seek help from the Brazilian footballer Socrates, his Greek philosopher namesake, Friedrich Nietzsche, the Chicago Bulls, the Lakota tribe, England's women's football team, the inmates of a Mississippi Delta prison, and many more.

In Part II, I grapple with the purpose and meaning of football (and life) as well as why we need change in our world and how we might go about achieving it. As critique comes before creation, we need to delve into and understand where we truly stand as a society. The literature of Albert Camus, Ursula Le Guin, Fyodor Dostoevsky, and Elie Wiesel meets the missed penalty of a Dane, the dribbling of a young Zapatista and the countless goals of Messi. The outline of an alternative football philosophy is traced here, revealing that football will either prop up a collapsing society or help change it.

In Part III, I discuss how the world can change through resistance and creation, on and off the pitch. With the help of educators, artists, psychologists, researchers, philosophers, comedians, footballers, and Formula 1 drivers, I imagine what a new football would look like in a new world. How can we create the football (and world) we want, within the football (and world) we wish to overcome?

Vasilis Kostakis,
Ioannina, Greece, July 2024

PART I
What is football?

1
Football is art

Socrates (1954–2011) was the captain of, perhaps, the best national team that never won the World Cup: the 1982 team from Brazil that competed in Spain. This team was brimming with talent, but their beautiful football was defeated by the opportunistic football of the Italian team, which went on to win the championship that year. Socrates played (1978–1984) for the Brazilian club Corinthians where he became famous for his opposition to the dictatorship of the country. Along with his teammates and many others at the club, he created the 'Democracia Corinthiana' movement to show that a truly democratic world is possible in football and beyond (this is explored further in Part III of this book). Socrates studied medicine alongside his dazzling football career. Beyond being a footballer, doctor, and activist, Socrates viewed himself as an artist as well. Football was his art.

'The tragedy of defeat rendered our struggle indelible'

In July 2010, artist Daniel Devlin met Socrates to talk about art and football. Before the conversation begins in earnest, Socrates raises his hand over two beers and, with slow, graceful movements, lights his interlocutor's cigarette. I am a staunch anti-smoker and do not drink either. I could not stand being in a room with such shameless smokers. Nevertheless, sparking a conversation this way seems, even to me, ritualistic. Perhaps deep down I am a well-repressed smoker. Devlin's and

Socrates's moves are effortless. So is their manner of speech. I cannot decide what it is they enjoy most: the cigarette, the beer, or the conversation? I suppose it's the mix of the three. I envy that.

Their videotaped conversation is split into different frames. Often the shot abruptly cuts away and the next one begins. I think about what might transpire in-between, away from our prying eyes when the camera is not recording. Maybe they're just enjoying their drinks and cigarettes in silence, staring at the ceiling. Time spent gazing into the distance is never time wasted. It is a prerequisite for a good chat.

What does beautiful football mean, asks Devlin. 'I think football is a sport that has an intimate relationship with dance', Socrates replies, eliciting a quizzical look from Devlin. 'There are choreographies, not always well-rehearsed, but … they have a content of physical expression that is much more interesting than the game itself', he explains. Football, he continues, 'is perhaps the only sport where the worst team may be the winner. It is fascinating … The ugly wins over the beautiful'.

'If you try comparing football to painting: [in painting] you can have beautiful brush strokes … [and] you try to communicate meaning. In football, the meaning might be scoring a goal', Devlin comments. 'I don't know', replies Socrates, preparing for one of his finest (verbal) volleys. 'I see football as art. Today most people see football as a competition, a confrontation, a war between two polar opposites. But, to start with, football is a great art form. It's like a group of painters in the same studio trying to do the same thing. Some will be noticed for one kind of talent, others for another. But in the end, the audience is enticed fundamentally because of this art, because of this physical expression that is part of the game'.

'If we think of architecture', Devlin says, 'there's a beauty in functionality, some modern architecture is very beautiful because you can see that it's very simple and functional. And if I think of Mourinho's football – I'm sure you don't think it's beautiful football – there's a functionality which I find very beautiful'. Socrates might have been expecting a reference to Mourinho's football, for whom that year had ended with a treble (three winning titles in one year) with Inter Milan. Mourinho's cynical football is somewhat similar to Italy's football, which knocked Brazil out of the World Cup semi-finals in 1982. Football of expediency.

Socrates replies: 'Every kind of art is an expression of a certain culture. Obviously, there are clear differences between how, for example, a German team and a Brazilian team express themselves. Even today, with such communication and cultural interconnection, there are still many essential differences because we are beings with extremely diverse characteristics and with very distinct views of the world'.

Mourinho's football and Italy's football in 1982 is art for Socrates. But they coalesce into a culture that does not represent him. It's like a professionally orchestrated and recorded rendition of an old favourite song. Without the noisy imperfections of the reel-to-reel – an outdated recording technology – and analogue microphones. The re-recording of the song does the job but lacks that spark to move listeners the way the original might have. Like Brazil did in 1982, albeit, without lifting the cup.

'In the game you played against Italy, a draw would've qualified Brazil ... But you didn't play only to win, you played for playing. You wanted to win the game by playing beautiful football', Devlin comments. 'That game', replies Socrates, 'was the greatest game of the World Cup. And Italy also played extremely well too ... The truth is that Brazil was really enchanting ... Perhaps the tragedy of our having lost that game is one of the things that made it unforgettable. The imponderability that football provides us with'.

Devlin agrees and comments that 'the most beautiful team didn't win, but that's probably not the most important thing'. Socrates crosses his arms, smiles, and proclaims 'Yeah, I think winning is nothing'. Then he gets serious, 'We are talking about art and what is fundamental in art is expressing it. It's what art is for you. Now, whether it sells or not does not depend on you any more. You show what you have. It's not the victory that matters. It's not success that matters. It's not the beauty that matters. It's the content that matters ... In reality, those who seek only victory are seeking conformity. Those who seek art are doing it for themselves and to show the world who they are'. The conversation ends there, at least in front of the camera. Socrates laughs, gives Devlin a friendly pat on the shoulder and then stands up. To leave? Grab another beer perhaps? Only Socrates, Devlin, and the people behind the camera know.

A year after this encounter, Socrates dies, defeated by alcohol. After all, he wasn't playing to win. He was only interested in presenting his art. He was like a candle, burning fast and producing an intense light. This book aims to capture that light and use it to show the way to devotees of football as well as all the arts.

2
The football gods are dead

The Brazilian footballer Socrates is named after the, perhaps more famous, philosopher. The latter lived about 2400 years earlier and was a controversial figure in his time. He attracted the interest of the Athenians, especially the youth. He engaged in discussions all over the city, with people of all social classes and did not accept money from his students. Socrates was indifferent to daily pleasures, neglecting his appearance. He walked barefoot and had only one garment. Unlike Brazilian Socrates, he drank in moderation. In 399 BC, around the age of 70, Socrates was accused of impiety and of corrupting the youth. After a one-day trial, he was sentenced to death. He refused offers from friends to help him escape, drank the hemlock and died.

'Poets don't know what they're saying'

During his testimony, Socrates did not address the judges with the customary respect expected at the time. He reserved this for those who voted for his acquittal only. This way, Socrates showed his intention not to flatter the judges. He did not deem them all fitting for the task. Socrates attempted to both apologise for and refute the charges. He defended his philosophy and recounted encounters with various social groups. He talked, among other things, about poets, and in doing so he also spoke, without knowing it, about football too:

> That showed me in an instant that not by wisdom do poets write poetry, but by a sort of genius and inspiration; they are like diviners or soothsayers who also say many fine things, but do not understand the meaning of them. And the poets appeared to me to be much in the same case.

Socrates tells us that it is not wisdom that allows poets to create, but a kind of instinct. A God-given inspiration like that of the prophets who deliver sublime messages without fully comprehending them. It is the divine or a muse that allows an artist to make art. That is why some footballers who make art by scoring sometimes look up to the heavens. They thank God for their goals (and sometimes for the millions they make). But does God get involved with the scoring of goals?

Friedrich Nietzsche (1844–1900) was both an admirer and critic of Socrates' philosophy. Nietzsche emphatically stated that 'God is dead'. Inspiration is not God-given. God does not write poetry. God does not score goals. If we accept the death of God or the gods, 'our hearts overflow with gratitude, astonishment, presentiment and expectation', Nietzsche writes, 'At last the horizon seems open ... our ships can at last put out to sea in face of every danger ... our sea, again lies open before us; perhaps never before did such an "open sea" exist'.

I am not an atheist; I am agnostic. That is, I know not whether God or gods exist and I don't particularly care either. But as a scientist, I do study how people create art, goals, and other things. My work leads me to believe Nietzsche's view is correct and Socrates' is wrong. The art of football, like all human expression, is neither God-inspired nor God-given. When a player scores a goal, they must turn their gaze to the team, the bench, and the stands. Never upwards; always to the side. They should thank those who created the art of football, those who built the pitches, and those who planted the grass upon which they now dance. They should shout: 'The football gods are dead. We are the only ones left. We always dance together, score together, create together!' And so the open sea may appear before us.

3
We always dance together

The closest ocean to where I live is the Atlantic. Crossing it now, I choose not to go to South America, the land of beautiful football, but further up north and to the NBA (National Basketball Association). Why is the NBA featured in a book about football you may ask? It will help me explain how the art of football along with other sporting art is created. The NBA is one of the most popular and profitable sports leagues in the world. The Chicago Bulls of the 1990s are, perhaps, the greatest basketball team of all time. And their star, Michael Jordan, is considered by many to be the GOAT (Greatest of All Time). Rarely, in a team sport, is there such a broad consensus on who the greatest actually is.

The story of the 1990s Bulls is told in the smash-hit documentary series *The Last Dance*. Its popularity reflects the appeal of Jordan and the Bulls beyond sports. In fashion, music, and film. *The Last Dance* was scheduled to be released in the summer of 2020. However, because of the coronavirus pandemic, Netflix and ESPN decided to air the documentary earlier, as during the first lockdown, with stadiums closed, fans were hungry for spectacle.

'Mitakuye Oyasin'

The start of the 1997–1998 season finds the Bulls having claimed five championships in the last seven years. Management realised that several of the team's players were at the end of their most productive years. Therefore, it was deemed necessary to radically restructure the team to remain competitive. However, juggernaut players like Jordan and Scottie Pippen, as well as coach Phil Jackson, were opposed to such a restructuring.

Jordan argues that the Bulls players were entitled to defend last season's title. The decision to restructure was, he tells the interviewers, disrespectful to those who made the club commercially and athletically successful. But who really made the club successful? For Jordan, things are clear: 'I would never let someone who's not putting on a uniform and playing each and every day dictate what we do on the basketball court ... the team is much bigger than the 15 players. Those guys who work in the front office, they are good people, but the most important part of the process is the players'. So, is it the players or the clubs that win championships? Who should be credited with excellence in basketball, football, or any art form?

When Jerry Reinsdorf became the Bulls' major shareholder and chairperson in 1984, the club was not doing well either athletically or commercially. At the start of the 1985–1986 season, Jerry Krause (1939–2017), by then a talent scout, became the Bulls' General Manager. Shortly before, in 1984, Jordan had joined the Bulls after studying and playing at North Carolina State University in Chapel Hill, USA. Jordan says he was not keen on becoming a professional athlete. It was his coach at university who convinced him to do so. In his first year in the NBA, Jordan showed his unparalleled talent and was voted best young player of the year. Over the following 15 years, Jordan would go on to win six championships and be named the league's Most Valuable Player five times.

Once he took over management, Krause proceeded with a radical restructuring of the team. In 1985, he replaced the head coach with an assistant coach, tasked with implementing a new innovative, for the time, offensive strategy. Phil Jackson, who would later go on to win six championships as the Bulls' head coach, was hired by Krause as an assistant coach. Krause insisted on Jackson's hiring even though the latter did not have an impressive resume. As Reinsdorf put it, 'Krause started Phil Jackson's NBA coaching career ... If that hadn't happened, you never would have heard of Phil Jackson'. By 1987, Krause brought in Scottie Pippen, a then-unknown player from Central Arkansas State University, to the fold. Pippen would later become a key pillar of the Bulls' dynasty.

Let's get back to our question: Do players or clubs win championships? Shortly ahead of the 1997–1998 season, Krause stated that 'players don't win championships, organizations do'. This infuriated Jordan and drove a wedge between the players and management. Krause later clarified that he meant that it is not the players and coaches alone who win the championships, but the entire club. 'I do sincerely believe that organizations, as a whole, win', Krause held this view for at least five years before his feud with Jordan erupted. Here's what he said when the Bulls were winning their second championship in 1992: 'It starts with Jerry, and it goes down all the way to Joe Lee, our clubhouse guy who's been here 25 years. It's an organisation thing, and that's what it's all about'. Jordan, however, insists that 'the most important part of the process is the players'.

In *The Last Dance* we see Jordan emphasise how important Pippen and Jackson were, not only to the Bulls' success, but to his own development and career. 'Pippen', Jordan admits, 'helped me so much in the way that I approached the game, the way I played the game. Whenever they speak Michael Jordan, they should speak Scottie Pippen'. Pippen and Jackson had not accomplished much before they were spotted and brought to the Bulls by Krause. Even Jordan, who once said he wouldn't play for any coach other than Jackson, was sceptical when Krause upgraded Jackson from assistant to head coach. So, Jackson, Jordan, Pippen, the other players, and the management that picked them, even the 'clubhouse guy', who kept the uniforms crisp and the ball dry, all made the Bulls what they were.

Professional athletes reach such dizzying highs, not only due to sheer talent and effort but a multitude of other reasons. They owe to their families, their opponents, the schools they studied and first played at, those who played and developed the sport before them, the fans who co-developed the team's philosophy, those providing the capacity to play the sport peacefully as well as those dealing with any injury, those in charge of communication, strategy, negotiations. The list goes on.

There is nothing more toxic than the myth of the self-made man/entrepreneur, whose success is the result of hard work and talent alone. At the core of the message this book is trying to convey is the notion that all the goals, the dunks, the three-pointers, the music that defines us, the vaccines we invent, and the technologies that make our lives easier, are all social products.

The Bulls documentary is rich with references to the institutions, ideas, and people that made Jordan and others what they are. The importance of social contribution cannot be captured in financial terms or numbers. It has no inherent value in the marketplace. That's why it remains invisible. But it's still very important in the operation of the NBA, the Premier League, Hollywood, the Stock Exchange, and pretty much any other organisation. Collective institutions, such as public health, exist to prevent and absorb such risks, even unforeseen crises like a pandemic. For example, in 2020 the NBA season was interrupted by the COVID-19 pandemic. If the medical staff, scientists, and other relevant professionals did not help contain the pandemic, if society itself did not help stop the spread of the infection, then neither the presidents of the NBA teams nor the players would have been able to compete. Yet this contribution is not highlighted in the contract of a professional athlete or Hollywood star.

Clubs cannot exist without players and players cannot compete without clubs. The sporting (and commercial) value of each league is produced because of this coexistence. In the same way, the league cannot exist in a world without fields, balls, sports education, or those that designed and developed the sport. All relationships and interactions between players, coaches, and agents make sense within a community. Therefore, no league can exist without the community. Everything is produced collectively, in common.

This idea lies at the heart of the Lakota, a North American native tribe. The Lakota philosophy deeply affected Jackson's coaching approach. Jackson, who after the Bulls won five more championships with the Lakers, published a book discussing his inspiration. He combined Lakota spirituality with the principles of Buddhism to instil players with the value of collectivity and solidarity. To show them that the team is more than the sum of its parts. To help players such as Jordan, Pippen, and the late Kobe Bryant reach their full potential through teamwork and coexistence.

'*Mitakuye Oyasin*' is an emblematic phrase within Lakota culture. It translates as everything and everyone is interconnected. People, trees, plants, rocks, insects, and other animals. All work together to form life as we know it. All value is produced collectively and we must all realise this. 'Being aware is more important than being smart', Jackson writes in his autobiography, his fingers unable to fit the eleven championship rings he has won in the NBA. Perhaps we could say the eleventh ring belongs to society that made it all possible.

4
We always sing together

Let's linger in North America just a little longer. The land where European colonialists, after decimating Indigenous populations, transported millions of slaves from Africa. The ancestors of the Lakota lived in the Mississippi region where, a few centuries later, Black slaves would be packed into the infamous Parchman Farm prison. After the American Civil War, around the end of the nineteenth century, the economy of Southern states was devastated. Former slaves were theoretically free. Now that slavery was abolished, where would white Southern landowners and businessmen procure free labour? The solution was an absurdly strict and racist legal framework. At the slightest misstep, Black people would return as incarcerated 'criminals' to offer their free labour. Different punishments were meted out depending on skin colour.

In 1901, Parchman Farm, the most brutal prison in the American South, was established. It was located conveniently adjacent to cotton fields where the Black prisoners would work from morning until night-time. That was 15 hours in temperatures that sometimes exceeded 37 degrees Celsius. The state of Mississippi saved millions of dollars from the labour of incarcerated former slaves. Back then, it was normal for people to die working in miserable conditions just to grow cotton for the landowner. Today they die building stadiums in Qatar. You may call that progress. The inmates/workers at Parchman Farm would occasionally sing. It's their songs I wish to tell you about.

'Well-a, whosoever told it, He told a dirty lie, babe'

Alan Lomax (1915–2002) was an American ethnomusicologist – a song hunter – known for his outdoor recordings, particularly folk music created and played by the people (music that was not 'signed' by one creator). Folk songs, jokes, fairy tales, cooking recipes, and traditional children's games are typical examples of co-creation. There is a special freedom that characterises these artefacts. Each and every person becomes a songwriter, a musician, and a co-creator. There is no copyright to prevent creation and no artificial barriers to hinder something that is inherently free. But how can one speculate when goods such as culture and knowledge are in abundance? Restriction is a prerequisite for maximising profit. You can distil art in bottles and sell it like water. Maybe one day soon we'll bottle air too.

Folk songs spread through word-of-mouth across spatial and cultural borders. This freedom imbues the lyrics and music with the history and traditions of a place. The values and emotions of people, while linking them to local dances and customs. It is a form of intercultural communication. The medium is art and the message is the particular local reality. Folk songs typically branch out into hundreds of versions. They uniquely adapt different linguistic idioms, musical styles, and historical and cultural traits. They are free cultural goods, shaped by small and large contributions from countless authors who have shared their common knowledge and experience over many generations.

During the 1930s and 1940s, Lomax documented the musical culture of the American South. The Mississippi Delta is the place where African music intertwines with the suffering of oppressed Black people. It's where blue-collar men and women, free or imprisoned, work day and night, and where blues music is born. Blues music, or simply the blues, is the basis of many modern music genres like jazz, rock, R'n'B, and soul. In 1947, Lomax visited Parchman Farm prison. He recorded slaves singing while they worked. By singing, the slaves created a sense of camaraderie during their forced labour. When singing together perhaps the pain and fatigue eased a little. When pain is shared it diminishes and when joy is shared it grows. But here, they sang about their misery:

> Well, it's early in the morn', in the morning, baby …
> Well, it's I have a misery, …
> Well-a, whosoever told it, that he told a
> He told a dirty lie, babe …
> Well-a takes a-rock – takes a gravel to make a
> To make a solid road

We established earlier that the Chicago Bulls of the 1990s would not come to be without the convergence of players, administrators, other clubs, stadiums, coaches, kit managers, those who developed the sport, fans, universities, public officials, the Lakota philosophy, and so much more. So too Elvis, the Beatles, the Rolling Stones, Johnny Mitchell, Joan Baez, Billie Eilish (I am down with the youth) and so many other successful (and multi-millionaire) artists would not be who they are if it weren't for the art of oppressed Black people (which itself was based on the art of other cultures in a different time and place).

'The stuff of folklore, the orally transmitted wisdom, art and music of the people', writes Lomax, 'can provide ten thousand bridges across which men of all nations may stride to say, You are my brother'. Yet some 'brothers' take the credit and money while owing much to the 'family'. These few select brothers and sisters did not appear in a vacuum but within a social context. They did not create their art from scratch. Cristiano Ronaldo doesn't score alone. Sometimes he gets a good assist, he's in the right position because he's football smart, someone won the penalty, someone coached him, took care of him, taught him the sport, invented the sport. So let's take it home, where the art of modern football was born.

5
It came home

Football, as we know it today, was first introduced in England. The original regulations were published at the end of the nineteenth century: first by Cambridge University and then by the oldest active football club, Sheffield FC. With the establishment of the Football Association of England in 1863, we have official regulations. That's why England is considered the home of modern football.

However, England's home team has not had much success at the international level. The only trophy the national team has won is the World Cup in 1966, and that competition took place in England. Since then, England has failed to 'bring home' a trophy. Or has it?

In 1966, it was illegal for women to participate in competitive sports. However, 56 years later, England's women's national football team played in the final of the European Championships and brought it home. Or rather it stayed home as it had done in 1966. As both times Germany were the opponents and the match was played in a packed Wembley Stadium.

'Women are emotional, that's why they concede more goals'

On the last Sunday of July 2022, the women's team (I wonder why 'women's' is a requirement in sports, while 'men's' is always implied) won the European Championship in extra time. Five weeks before, the US Supreme Court overturned a 50-year-old ruling that ensured abortion was legal nationwide. Millions of women in the US are now very likely to lose the right to have an abortion. Patriarchy is going nowhere it seems.

A few months earlier, in April 2022, the Northern Ireland women's national team lost 5–0 to the English team. Northern Ireland's then-coach, Kenny Shields, in the press conference following the match, states: 'In the women's game ... if you go through the patterns, when a team concedes a goal they concede a second one within a very short period of time ... Because girls and women are more emotional than men ... and that's an issue that we have – not just Northern Ireland – but all the countries have that problem'. Immediately afterwards, Ian Wright, a former footballer and current sports commentator, shared a photo on Twitter of himself playing in an Arsenal shirt and tears flowing. Which brings to mind Paul Gascoigne's sobs at the 1990 World Cup in Italy. In Shields' words, who apologised afterwards, we see well-established stereotypes. The stereotype of men is that they are hardened or stoic and therefore don't (shouldn't) cry. This is perhaps why women typically feel more comfortable than men in expressing their feelings. We are all emotionally vulnerable sometimes and crying is a natural response we are all entitled to.

I do not intend to examine the roots of patriarchy and misogyny here. There are excellent studies that do a far better job at this than I ever could. Football does not exist and does not evolve in a vacuum. It evolves within society. It can be argued that football is a microcosm of society. Where class, gender, and all kinds of inequalities plague and define the lives of billions of people, football is not unaffected by this. Football has the potential to create a different world. What kind of world and how it could come to be will be discussed in the other two parts of this book. For now, let's spend some more time exploring the relationships that permeate every human creative process.

Women's contributions to society are often unseen. According to the traditional patriarchal model, the man brings in the money and is thus he is the one who holds the power. Just like the football player who scores the most goals and gets the most glory and, usually, money. The woman does the housework and raises children. At least in the 'first' world, the situation is no longer like that, one might say. In 2011 the value of unpaid work for women worldwide was estimated at about $8 trillion compared to $3 trillion for men. With the coronavirus pandemic, women's contribution increased even more. That is because the need to care for children and the elderly as well as household chores intensified.

Fédération Internationale de Football Association (FIFA) provides fewer resources to the women's national teams. In the US, however, we have seen a historic development in professional 'soccer' (as they call it over there). In May 2022, the unions of the men's and women's national teams agreed to share the FIFA money equally. Where the constitutional right to abortion was abolished and several steps backwards were taken, this was a small step forward. We are slowly staggering forward.

6
So what is football anyway?

In principle, football is a physical expression. It is a movement in space, with or without the ball; a movement that is more or less harmonious; movement, premeditated or instinctual; movement as part of a plan that seeks victory or expression in itself; movement, violent or aethereal. The adoption of one extreme or the other – or a nuanced in-between – characterises the values and culture of those who create football content. Every movement or touch of the ball is a brushstroke; every match, a painting; every season, a gallery exhibition. Several exhibitions give us a football movement, a philosophy; a, more or less, distinct identity. Football is a cultural expression. It is art.

Football marries competition with cooperation. Players of the same team, when training, compete but also cooperate. During a match, they cooperate with each other and compete with the players of the opposing team. Together they produce spectacle and art. I maintain that football, like any art form, is primarily a cooperative process. Just like nature.

We now know that the evolution of species is determined more by cooperation and less by competition. Our cells are the result of cooperation between microorganisms over billions of years. Trees communicate and cooperate underground, through their roots and other organisms like fungi. For example, shorter evergreen trees are covered by the foliage of taller deciduous trees in the summer. Unable to gather enough sun to photosynthesise, they need help. The taller trees send them the necessary nutrients underground. In winter, however, the taller deciduous trees shed their leaves and now it is they who are unable to photosynthesise. Then the evergreens, which now see the sun, reciprocate. The fungi, for all the work they do, withhold a percentage of the nutrients they carry to make sure the whole ecosystem stays healthy.

It is difficult to understand the complexity of creation and evolution. Trees, fungi, and humans exist in their forests, their ecosystems, and their societies. They are not units but parts of a larger system. Nothing – at least from the creation of the universe onwards – grows in a void. There is no parthenogenesis.

However, speaking of human societies, we are not all equally talented at everything. As we will see later, not all people have the same privileges and affordances. We don't all make the same decisions. We don't all take the same risks. Certainly, the scorer makes a critical contribution. But they couldn't produce art without the team. The team would have no reason to exist without the opposing teams. Teams would not exist without the sport. None of it would exist without society. Everything is created in common.

PART II
What world do we want?

7
We all kicked a ball once

To answer how we can change the world with a ball, it is important to explain why we play football. Or, put differently, why we create art. Art is a basic human feature or perhaps a need. We all, to a greater or lesser extent, create art. We all need to express ourselves. We all painted, sang, or danced once. We all kicked a ball.

The primary function of art, then, is self-expression. Through art, we externalise our feelings. We paint or play football because we enjoy the process itself. We make art for art's sake. The painting or goal is the destination. What is most interesting is the journey. The game. By making art we take a step closer towards harmony or balance with ourselves. By making art we confront the mystery of our existence. What does it all mean?

We enter this world without an instruction manual. Why do we exist instead of not existing? From our depressingly limited understanding of the universe, non-existence is the norm (at least for now). Life on our planet is an exception. And that exception (at least the human species) is aware of its own existence. How tragic and fascinating at the same time! We look at our own reflection and ask ourselves, 'Why do I live? Why do I face such hardship and then perish? What is the meaning of it all?' A mystery with no answer that has been driving our creativity since our species achieved awareness.

'Mystery is the source of all true art'

'The most beautiful thing we can experience is the mysterious. It is the source of all true art and all science. He to whom this emotion is a stranger, who can no longer pause to wonder and stand rapt in awe, is as good as dead: his eyes are closed'. I'm fairly certain this is a quote from Albert Einstein. Struggling for self-expression can give meaning not only to the person creating it but also to those who experience their art. Therefore the second purpose and function of art is communication, emotion, and meaning-making. Children draw to express a feeling, an idea, a thought. By sharing their drawings with a parent they establish a communion. Meaning is shared.

To share art is to communicate at a fundamental level. By communicating we grow closer. We share the pain of our (futile?) existence and this relieves the burden somewhat. We share feelings and thoughts and these create meaning. When the team celebrates a goal with their fans or even when they cope with defeat, shared meaning is created.

We cannot, however, answer the great mystery of existence. But we can exorcise (even for a moment) the anxiety and psychological vicissitudes that may overwhelm us by watching, listening to, and interpreting a work of art. By participating in artistic drama. A piece of music, a play, a painting, a sculpture, a football match. For this catharsis to take place, art must succeed in touching us, in moving us. What moves us? 'Beauty', footballer Socrates would answer. 'Everything is beautiful when it serves its purpose well', his ancient namesake would add.

What is the purpose of football? A spectacular match full of unexpected moments and thrilling goals is certainly nice. But is there a beauty in a strong defence? In discipline, in the closing down of spaces, in scrapping for the ball, in the sloppy fall from over-exertion, in failure, in the reduced stamina of older players? And does the meaning found in the art of football make our world a better place? Should it make it better, in principle? And if so, what does a better world mean? Better for whom? In the following chapters, I will attempt to answer these questions, often with the help of an art form not so unrelated to football after all: literature.

8
The one who always kicked the can

Albert Camus (1913–1960) was a French-Algerian philosopher, writer, and journalist. He was also a goalkeeper for the Racing Universitaire d'Alger youth team from the age of 15 to 17 when he had to quit as he suddenly started spitting up blood from having contracted tuberculosis. Football never ceased to fascinate him. Like Gonzalez, in Camus' *The Plague*, who never missed the chance to kick a tin can when it appeared in front of him. In 1959, a year before his death, Camus said in an interview that his two 'real universities' were the theatre and football. This rowdy and physical drama based around an errant leather ball made Camus's lungs swell with life. It was through the excitement and passion of the match that he learned solidarity, teamwork, and perseverance in the face of futility. He discovered aspects of himself that he was unaware of and had to tame: the drive for revenge, selfishness, jealousy.

On 16 October 1957, Camus was dining in the Latin Quarter of Paris, where some of the most famous universities in France are located. Suddenly, a young man from Camus's publishing house interrupted to break the news: the Swedish Academy had awarded Camus the Nobel Prize for Literature. A week later he was being interviewed for French television. The interview did not take place in a fancy studio but in the Parc de Princes amongst 35,000 fans watching the match between Racing Paris and Monaco. There are direct or indirect references to football in most of Camus's works. How can an intellectual grappling with the complex issues of existence, revolution, and so much more, love such a simple sport?

'Life is absurd! Let's play some ball'

What is more absurd than 22 people chasing a ball around a rectangular space for 90 minutes, trying to get the ball to cross a line painted on the ground? For Camus, what is more absurd is life itself. If we look at our lives over time, is chasing a career, a car, love, or a ball really that different? After 100, 1000, and 10,000 years – time that is insignificant on a cosmic scale – our existence will be forgotten. It will be as if we had never lived at all. 'We long for happiness' but we always receive the 'absurd silence of the world', Camus writes.

And what should we do about it? End it all? Camus urges us to look at life with cold logic. Life itself has no meaning. We start from nothingness and march towards nothingness. But we can create meaning. Revolution against all forms of injustice and exploitation is, for Camus, a constructive way to make sense of our lives. 'I rebel, therefore we exist', he tells us, emphasising coexistence as a means of signification. Whether the revolution succeeds or fails is utterly irrelevant from the point of view of cosmic time. In the end, all will perish. However, by fighting for less injustice and exploitation we may leave a better world for future generations. They too will struggle – probably achieving very little in their individual lives – but cumulatively enough that after 50, 100, and 200 years the world will be a better place for most creatures on the planet.

One of Camus's favourite books was *The Brothers Karamazov*, Dostoevsky's last novel. Camus seems to embrace the words of Ivan Karamazov when he explains where he finds meaning: 'Sticky spring leaves, the blue sky – I love them, that's all! Such things you love not with your mind, not with logic, but with your insides'. Football is to Camus what spring leaves and the blue sky are to Ivan Karamazov. A place where he can be free from other thoughts. Free as a child in the company of other children. What matters is self-expression as part of a collective: 'No matter how hard the struggle, no matter how difficult life is, we will face it together'. So, with a ball, one can express oneself, co-exist, communicate, and even change the world.

Two years before his death, Camus bought a house in Lourmarin, a mountain village north of Marseille. He would have coffee after matches with players of the local football team, which he supported financially. On New Year's Day 1960, his publisher and friend Michel Gallimard offered to drive him to Paris. The car skidded off the road and hit a tree. Camus was killed instantly. He was buried in the mountains of Lourmarin. His coffin was carried by the teary-eyed footballers of the Lourmarin team. 'However hard life may be, let us bear this burden together', they might have said.

9
The hallowed lost penalty

From the mountains of Lourmarin, we jump south, to the mountains of Italy, where in the 1940s the partisans fought the fascists singing 'Fischia il vento' – a revolutionary folk song. It was written to lift the spirits of partisans and keep them united in the face of adversity. So, it served a specific purpose. As did Picasso's famous painting, *Guernica*, with its mutilated appendages and desperate faces. Picasso, during the Spanish Civil War (1936–1939), sent a striking message by capturing the inhumanity and brutality of war. Some works of art embody more clear political messages than others. This is one of those.

In football, the missed penalty by Morten Wieghorst held a very specific message. In 2003, Denmark faced Iran in a friendly match. Just before the end of the first half, a fan blew a whistle which confused an Iranian defender who had the ball in his own penalty box. As he mistakenly thought the referee had signalled halftime, he picked up the ball with his hands. Consequently, the referee awarded a penalty in favour of Denmark. Wieghorst took it, deliberately missing the kick with the agreement of coach Morten Per Olsen. Denmark lost 1–0. This moment of art has gone down in history. For me, it celebrates justice and shows that winning shouldn't be everything.

Most of the time, of course, interpretation lies with those who look, listen, and feel art. Another moment that has been indelibly etched in collective memory is the 'Hand of God' goal (1986). This incident occurred during the quarter-final match between Argentina and England in the 1986 FIFA World Cup in Mexico City. Six minutes into the second half, with the score tied at 0–0, Maradona leapt to challenge the English goalkeeper Peter Shilton for a mis-hit clearance. Despite being much shorter, Maradona reached the ball first, using his left hand to guide it into the net. The referee, unaware of the handball, allowed the goal to stand. The goal was improvised and many considered it symbolic revenge for the Falklands War between Argentina and Great Britain (1982), a brief but bitter conflict over the disputed Falkland Islands (known as the Malvinas in Argentina) that had ended just four years prior. In post-match interviews, Maradona cryptically described the goal as scored 'a little with the head of Maradona and a little with the Hand of God', giving birth to its enduring moniker.

But there is another way read to it: 'the Hand of God' sends the opposite message to that of Wieghorst's missed penalty. It does not create a better world. In the crucible of Wieghorst's decision lays a kernel of selflessness, a triumph of moral rectitude over the rigidity of written edicts. It was a stark contrast to the so-called 'Hand of God', an act wherein the breach of rules was rationalised by a warped intertwining of football and the machinations of statecraft. I have my own values, perceptions, and beliefs. These have formed a prism through which I interpret the world and art. As have those who through art express their values and concerns. In this chapter, I want to talk about the task of the creator to bring people together in a deep and meaningful way. About their duty to take a stand.

> 'How can the world remain silent in the face
> of something like this?'

Elie Wiesel (1928–2016) was a Jewish author and winner of the Nobel Peace Prize (1986). One of his best-known works is *The Night*, based on his experiences as a prisoner in the Auschwitz and Buchenwald concentration camps. In *The Night* he writes about the 1930s and 1940s. A time when the world was confronted with the worst aspects of human nature. He writes about the concentration camps where Jews and other oppressed people were exterminated by the Nazis to increase their economy and power. 'Who would allow such crimes to be committed? How could the world remain silent?' asks a young Jewish boy in the book.

Today, a child from Syria, Palestine, or Myanmar might ask the same thing. Where the destitute of the world are living a tragedy whose catharsis never seems to come. It is the task of art to remind those who know and teach those who don't. Art must fight oblivion. 'Because if we forget', Wiesel writes, 'we are guilty, we are accomplices ... that is why I swore never to be silent whenever and wherever human beings endure suffering and humiliation'. Wiesel, however, was accused of remaining silent in the oppression of Palestinians. I do not know if he was rightly accused. But I do know that, especially today, it is necessary to take a stand. 'Neutrality helps the oppressor, never the victim', Wiesel continues.

Those who make art must take a stand. We are often lulled by the safety of neutrality and the languor of apathy. Perhaps because we fear losing our privileges, perhaps because we believe we live in the best world possible, or perhaps because we fear we are too small and incapable of facing injustice. 'Courage is as contagious as fear', American author Susan Sontag reminds us. Resisting injustice offers a profound sense of purpose to our lives. Rather than endorsing products like crisps, someone like Messi, often regarded as football's premier artist, could use his platform to address issues such as refugees, the climate crisis, and those who are plunging the world into poverty. As of the time of this writing, Messi holds the record for the most-liked photo on Instagram, while Cristiano Ronaldo boasts the largest Instagram following.

10
Messi stretches to infinity

'Wherever men or women are persecuted because of their race, religion, or political views, that place must – at that moment – become the centre of the universe', says Wiesel. I am writing these lines a few months after Messi, who made $122 million in 2021 alone, signed a $25 million contract for promoting tourism in Saudi Arabia. So Messi has certainly taken centre stage in a place where many are oppressed. And he has taken a stand too – probably without ever reflecting on it – a position in favour of the oppressors.

Oppression takes many forms. Oppressors may be those who, to maximise their profits, ravage the planet. They too may be using the dazzle of star players and the appeal of football to throw gold dust over a tragedy that is taking place. And what of those caught in the middle? The middle class of the 'free world'? While the Titanic's orchestra lulls us to sleep on the sinking ship, the powerful of the world ride in their luxury lifeboats.

'Come, the Amazon belongs to you'

After winning the World Cup in Qatar, the global press showered Messi with praise. At the age of 35, he was Argentina's most influential player, the ultimate leader, they wrote. In Argentina, millions of people glorify him. The state is considering printing banknotes featuring his face. Messi's Instagram account has broken all popularity records. In Rosario, his hometown, the statue of Che Guevara stares in amazement at a helicopter flying through the sky with a huge Messi jersey. Messi signifies the decadence and success of our culture in equal measure. He is successful because of the spectacle he has provided on the pitch and his stats are unimaginable. Titles, honours, goals, assists, games. Messi stretches to infinity.

The craze surrounding Messi is a symptom of our times. An era in which the success and prosperity of societies are measured in terms of 'growth', i.e. an increase in Gross Domestic Product (GDP). What can be measured and expressed in monetary units has value; what cannot is invisible and irrelevant. Perhaps the absurdity of capitalist 'growth' is greater than the absurdity of life, dear Camus. If parents look after their children instead of taking them to private nurseries, and if children look after their elderly parents instead of taking them to nursing homes, they are doing a disservice to 'growth'. They don't create numbers or value for the market. If we stop throwing away a third of the food we buy and distribute it to the most economically disadvantaged, we are doing a disservice to 'growth'. If we keep our fragile ecosystems intact, and our oceans clean, and do not drill for oil, we will be doing a disservice to 'growth'. War is good for 'growth'. Bomb everything, bomb it to dust, then have people work to death rebuilding it. 'Come multinational corporations, devour the Amazon', invited former Brazilian President Bolsonaro, 'while my friends Neymar, Ronaldinho, Rivaldo, and Robinho do leg and heel work for the drunken crowd'.

So is Messi the GOAT? Messi symbolises hard work and talent that is rightfully rewarded based on what he has achieved. In Part I, I tried to show that 'rightfully' is a relative term. He is rewarded with much more than he should be. Messi would not have made it without a plethora of social systems.

And he hasn't even contributed anything back, having scored from a deflection of paying tax as well. Messi is certainly one of the most talented footballers there has ever been. But I don't know if Messi is the GOAT or even if there is a point to such a discussion either way. What I do know is that Messi and his era need to be overcome. Cups, goals, and numbers are for statistics. We need artists who play for something greater than the cup and money. And if we don't have them, we need to create them.

11
The tragedy of our times

Let's shift from the GOAT to a rising star. On a Monday in September 2022, Paris Saint-Germain coach Christophe Galtier and Kylian Mbappé attended the team's press conference. A reporter asked why last weekend the team took a private jet for a short trip to a match in Nantes. It should be noted that Nantes is about two hours from Paris by high-speed train. That's when Galtier and Mbappé faced each other, with the up-and-coming possible GOAT bursting out laughing. They laughed together for 20 seconds. When Galtier regained his composure, he shot back as if having anticipated this question: 'This morning we talked about it with the company which organises our trips and we're looking into travelling on sand yachts'. Asked again about his views on the matter, Mbappé replied that he had no opinion. This was but one seemingly insignificant moment, but it revealed the tragedy of our century.

> 'It is difficult to understand something when your salary depends on you not understanding it'

We live in capitalism. What does that mean? That someone who belongs to the elite starts their morning with a huge amount of money at their disposal. And by evening they are usually even richer. The next day, of course, they must think up new ways to manage their new capital: will they reinvest it or consume it? Fierce competition forces them to reinvest, because if they don't, someone else will do it. Of course, the successful capitalist earns enough to reinvest the necessary funds to keep them in the game, while living an ultra-luxurious life with their yachts, private jets, private islands, and the list goes on.

The constant race to increase profitability is at the heart of capitalism: more, more, more, more and even more; it is never enough. The sky used to be the limit. No more. The space capitalist faces various challenges in his (it's usually a he) ascent to the skies. For example, sometimes workers suitable for a specific task are few and therefore well paid. Thus wages must drop or cheaper hands have to be procured. Also, the over-exploitation of nature enriches and expands the scope of 'growth'. With the help of technology, the distance between countries is reduced and the capitalists can find new raw materials, new labour, and new consumers. New needs are created along with new ways of consuming – often based on credit. You can use your plastic tokens to shop until the sun goes out (or more likely until our planet dies).

If our dear capitalists don't make enough, they create monopolies. 'Let's pool our assets, and control the market to continue growing safely!' If, after all this, enough capitalists don't make obscene profits, the system faces a serious crisis. Capitalists can't find profitable investment opportunities, their money stagnates and its value declines. 'We are too big to fail. Save us so that we, the saviour elites, may save you!' Massive unemployment, poverty, and destitution are observed in ever larger parts of the world's population.

Despite all this, many will argue that no other system has produced so much wealth. No system has ever produced so much destruction, others will counter. Capitalism produces more food than the world has ever imagined, but also so much hunger. So many new and so many empty houses. So many human rights, but also so many crimes against humanity. Worst of all, capitalism has led us to a profound, and probably inevitable, environmental disaster. In the name of maximising profits, the planet's ecosystems are treated as commodities begging to be exploited. This, then, is the tragedy of our times.

As Canadian journalist and author Naomi Klein asks, 'My mind keeps coming back to the question: What is wrong with us? What is really preventing us from putting out the fire that is threatening to burn down our collective house?'. Why is it easier to imagine the end of the world than the end of capitalism? If we do what is required to address the climate crisis and poverty, it will hurt the interests of 'an elite minority that has a stranglehold over our economy, our political process, and most of our major media outlets', she replies.

It is very tricky for Galtier and Mbappé to understand this tragedy because, as American writer Upton Sinclair eloquently observed, 'it is difficult to get a man to understand something, when his salary depends on his not understanding it'. In this case, look who is funding Paris Saint-Germain. How do they make their money? Which companies pay Mbappé to advertise their products and how do they make their money? Is it through underpaid labour and exploitation of natural goods? Is the transportation of their products polluting the planet? Is their business model based on over-consumption and fast fashion? One only needs to follow the money to understand.

12
When you're 4–0 down in the 89th minute, can you turn the tide?

Early in the 2020 pandemic, stadiums went silent. In 2050 many stadiums may not even exist. 'Around a quarter of professional stadiums in the top four leagues are under threat of annual flooding or actually being underwater by 2050', says author and sociologist David Goldblatt. The climate crisis is here (we brought it, in fact) to stay. Fires and floods are on the rise, destroying infrastructure and ecosystems and helping spread disease. Temperatures are rising, desertifying more and more parts of the planet. Droughts are devastating vast areas of cropland. We are all exposed to the consequences of the climate crisis, but the poorest are the most vulnerable. Do we have time to face this crisis? Many will say: 'Look how Qatar did at the 2022 World Cup. Look how well green Denmark has been doing. Climate neutrality is the solution' Are they right? Let's see.

> 'A climate Qatar-strophe unfolds before our very eyes'

First things first, what does 'climate neutrality' even mean? Climate neutrality is about shifting to a world with zero greenhouse gas emissions. Qatar aimed for the 2022 World Cup and all that entailed (from stadium construction to transportation) to have zero emissions. Zero ecological footprint. The World Cup would grow Qatar's economy without harming the environment. That is, what we call 'green growth'. So it's obvious why 'climate neutrality' is important. But is it feasible in an economy that constantly seeks to grow? In an economy where governments want GDP to grow every year? How would Qatar manage such a task?

The typical answer entails some mixture of high technologies. Smart, electric cars and buses, big wind turbines in the mountains and huge photovoltaic parks in the plains and deserts, robots in factories and on the streets. Everything will, somehow, turn green. Look at the green 'miracle' of Copenhagen or some other northern European city, the advocates of 'green growth' will say. What they fail to mention, intentionally or not, is that green 'miracles' do not consider the greenhouse gas emissions they cause in other parts of the world. If they did, they wouldn't be green at all.

Modern technologies are related to global wealth inequalities but also to the climate crisis. For example, an electric bus, like the ones roaming Qatar, hits the streets as a finished product. To get a shiny new smartphone, we pay for it online and it's at our doorstep a couple of days later. This monetary transaction masks the labyrinthine processes required for it to reach our hands. In truth, the manufacturing, maintenance, and disposal of modern technologies involve significant amounts of energy, toxic waste, and work in inhumane conditions. We do not think about how our phone was designed in the US, manufactured in China, Pakistan, and South Korea, with raw materials from the Congo, and shipped from China to Greece via two or three other countries. We do not care where it ends up when it's designed to break down after a couple of years.

Think of every modern technology that Qatar, Denmark, you, and I use. The green 'miracle' of Copenhagen is based on pollutants and often on child labour in other parts of the world, usually in Africa and South East Asia. Copenhagen is therefore not a climate-neutral city. Its sustainability is based on the misery of people and the destruction of local ecosystems far from 'green' Denmark. The supposed climate neutrality of the Qatar World Cup is at the expense of ecosystems elsewhere in the world. In the age of climate crisis, the local is global and the global is local. Everything is interconnected.

Further, those who advocate technology as the ultimate solution to the climate crisis are forgetting something. That the more efficient modern technologies are, the more we tend to use them. So instead of reducing pollutants, they increase. Qatar's electric bus uses less energy per kilometre. So now that it is cheaper, it is an opportunity to travel more kilometres per day. And some people, such as the super-rich of this earth, use technologies with environmental footprints millions of times larger than those of the average person. As we saw earlier, Mbappé's team travels from Paris to Nantes in a private jet. Therefore, at the end of the day, carbon dioxide emissions are increasing.

Another way of (supposedly) ensuring 'climate neutrality' is carbon offsets. For the World Cup in Qatar to be branded climate-neutral, carbon offsets were key. What does this mean? That one can buy the right to pollute. You pollute in Qatar, for example, and you go 'this is fine, I'm ok with this. I'll plant many trees elsewhere or build a photovoltaic park to compensate for the harm I've caused'. Something akin to the indulgences the Pope used to give out as absolution in the Middle Ages. Have you sinned? No problem. For ten gold coins, you've cleansed yourself and St Peter is laying out an ecological red carpet for you in heaven. Do these trade-offs work? Probably about as well as the indulgences did. It is very difficult to control where the money given, for example, by Qatar goes. There are many cases where offset projects have caused more problems in local ecosystems, especially where Indigenous populations live (e.g. Africa, Amazon).

How exactly do we measure the impact of offset projects? If one wishes to wash away their environmental sins by building a photovoltaic park somewhere in Africa, do they calculate the actual, global environmental footprint of building the park? If they do, the green offset projects will start going grey. A 2016 study found that 85 per cent of offset projects did not reduce carbon emissions. Since then, not much has changed. Another study in 2021 found that 90 per cent of the offset projects it reviewed did not deliver what was promised. For example, there was supposed to be a huge tree plantation project in Cambodia. Satellite images show that within a decade half of the trees planted had been destroyed while there was a commitment to preserve them. Naomi Klein has mused about how emissions offsets are like taking one step forward and one step back, at best we are standing still.

The Qatar World Cup was 'a climate Qatar-strophe' as an article in *Scientific American* notes. The 'greenwashing' of the Cup is dangerous because 'it gives the impression that we can build massive state-of-the-art stadiums ... and fly people from all over the world to watch football matches and that's somehow compatible with reaching climate targets', says Gilles Dufrasne, a researcher at Carbon Market Watch. The problem, then, is not technical; it is political. A political solution is needed, not a technological one. Modern technologies can certainly help. I'm not saying we should all go back to the caves or live by candlelight. However, the political context is crucial: who will lose some of their privileges for the sake of the many and the environment? How long will we tolerate the human misery inflicted to maximise the monetary gains of a few super-rich? The answers to these questions are political. Can football be a catalyst for wider social and political change? Before I answer, let's have one last dance because the mood has grown heavy.

13
The poor are poor because they make poor choices

Let's get back to *The Last Dance*. The documentary about the Chicago Bulls dynasty of the 1990s contains another story that is interesting not just as a sports anecdote but as commentary on inequality too. Everyone interviewed acknowledged the immense basketball value of Scottie Pippen. They also acknowledged that he was underpaid. At the start of the 1997–1998 season, Pippen was one of the top active players in the league. With the Bulls, he was second in scoring and rebounding. He led in assists and steals. But he was the sixth-highest-paid player in the club and 122nd in the entire NBA. Was it reasonable for him to feel wronged?

'You've made your bed'

In 1991, Pippen signed a seven-year, $18 million contract. Reinsdorf, the Bulls's president, recalls telling him, 'You may be selling yourself too short. It's too long a contract you're locking yourself in for'. Reinsdorf was right. As prominent sportswriter Rick Telander writes, 'if he [Pippen] had played it right, he could have made nine times that amount, ten times'. In the years that followed, not only did Pippen improve dramatically, but the economic value of the NBA overall skyrocketed. As he says, 'revenues went up, salaries went up'. But Reinsdorf was unmoved. Once a contract is signed 'I don't want to hear from you again. Don't come back in here, try to renegotiate'. As the Bulls' second-best player, Pippen's displeasure was intense.

In the summer of 1997, Pippen had the opportunity to have surgery during a dead period for the NBA. However, he decided to move his surgery to the beginning of the season. He didn't want to miss his summer vacation but also wanted retribution for the perceived injustice. Jordan believes that Pippen 'was wrong ... What Scottie was trying to do was trying to force management to change his contract ... I felt like Scottie was being selfish. Worrying about himself as opposed to what his word was to the organization as well as to the team'.

While Jordan came from a middle-class family, Pippen came from a poor family of twelve with two members, his father and a brother, who were wheelchair-bound. Pippen's family situation was such that he was not in a position to take big risks. What would happen if he was injured? He thus ended up with a safe but unprofitable deal for himself. Says Pippen: 'I had to take care of my people'. The circumstances under which Pippen decided to sign were quite different from Jordan's. To portray Pippen's misjudgement as his own fault is toxic.

This toxicity is crystallised in the myth of the 'self-made' man/entrepreneur. The successful and self-made man/entrepreneur is rewarded for making the right decisions. He (it's also usually a he) took big risks and thus big bonuses are justified. However, for some it is much easier to take risks without fear that failure will destroy them. They may have financial security from family or privileged access to certain institutions and infrastructure.

Therefore, Pippen's contract should not be seen simply as a private agreement between him and the club. But as just one moment in a complex system of value creation for himself, the club, the NBA, and society in general. The question now is whether it was reasonable for him to feel wronged. If one looks at the injustice against Pippen in the context of the NBA, then one can conclude that he was extremely underpaid.

For CNN's Brandon Tensley, this injustice is a reminder of the long-standing inequality that exists in the US regarding its Black population. Indeed, Matthew Miranda writes in *Jacobin*: 'The gap between working-class fans and millionaire players is no less a chasm than that between millionaire players and billionaire owners'. Miranda claims that Jordan, who in 15 years received a total of $93 million in earnings from the Bulls, and LeBron James, who in 15 years earned $237 million, are two of the lowest-paid players. He compares the earnings of Jordan and James to the earnings of their team owners. But his approach is skewed. First, Jordan and James made hundreds of millions from advertising. That revenue, as we saw above, would not exist if it weren't for their team, the NBA and society. Second, the gap between working-class fans and millionaire players is much wider than that between players and owners. The fundamental problem lies not in the players vs. owners dichotomy but in a generally flawed understanding of how value is generated.

In the 1990s, Pippen's average annual salary was $2.5 million, while the average annual salary of the US president was $0.2 million. Scientists, doctors, teachers, and other professionals received significantly less. Pippen was more than adequately paid. So were all the other players. The profits earned by the team presidents seem absurd because there is no recognition for the share of society's contribution. This is why so many professions are not paid rationally based on their contribution to society. Especially when compared to the salaries of CEOs, bankers, footballers, and otherwise famous people. The free market defines salaries in a myopic way. It comprehends only what is expressed in numbers. The complex and multifaceted reality is reduced to a number. Consequently, global inequality is caused and sustained by our failure to understand the contribution of many more factors to the success that few taste. However, global wealth inequality has other historical causes. So let's take a walk on the unseen side of the earth.

14
The tunnel to the other side of the earth

I am a father of two children. To explain the problems their generation is destined to face, I wrote the following children's story:

Zoe wants to play with her dad's phone. But her dad won't let her. 'I'm busy', he says. 'Go do some digging. Go and find some treasure. Put it in your bag and bring it back to me'. He gives her a bucket and a spade and starts talking on his phone again.

Zoe digs while her dad talks on his phone. You can find many treasures by digging! Here is a worm that likes to live in the soil. Here is some rusty metal. Here is an old piece of pottery.

Deeper still. Here are the roots of a big tree! 'I will not hurt them because the tree drinks water and eats its food through its roots', thinks Zoe. She carries on digging. Her dad is still on the phone. She gets to a part of the earth with big rocks that she has to dig out of the way, and then finds two beautiful red stones. 'I will carry them in my bag and start building a little red house with them'.

THE TUNNEL TO THE OTHER SIDE OF THE EARTH

What a huge tunnel Zoe has made while her dad is still on the phone! 'I will find what is hidden at the other end of the hole', she says to him. But he is not listening. She keeps digging, and digging, and digging. Then, suddenly, she sees light. Her head pops out into a strange place on the other side of the world. The sun is burning hot, and the air smells dusty, but look how many children are digging! And here, the parents dig too.

Zoe walks up to the child and asks: 'What kind of treasures are you looking for?' 'Copper and cobalt', the child answers. 'What games do you play with them?' Zoe asks. 'We do not play games', he says sadly. 'We sell them to the grown-ups on the other side of the world'.

'What do grown-ups do with your copper and cobalt?' Zoe asks. 'They make phones', the child answers and goes back to his digging. The child has no time for games. He must dig in the sun so that grown-ups can talk on the phone.

'This isn't fair', Zoe thinks, 'not fair at all!'. 'What is your name?' she asks the child. 'Beno', he says.

Beno and Zoe sit together and laugh. Zoe shows him the red stones from her bag, and they come up with a great idea! He will stop looking for copper and cobalt and instead look for coloured stones too. They will share them through the tunnel. They can share shovels and buckets too, and ideas. And then they will build wonderful houses with their friends at both ends of the tunnel ...

Zoe says goodbye to Beno, promising to see him the next day. Then she goes back through the tunnel, to tell her dad what she has discovered. Zoe pops her head out of the tunnel and sees that her dad isn't on the phone anymore. 'Where have you been Zoe?' he says, in a worried voice. Zoe tells him about Beno, and her dad looks thoughtful. 'After dinner, let's go through the tunnel and talk to Beno about building wonderful red houses', he says. And they do. And, for the rest of the day, her dad didn't use his phone at all.

When I read my children this tale, they bombarded me with questions that seemed obvious to a child. But not to an adult who has been brainwashed by mainstream economic thinking (even if one doesn't read economics – it suffices to follow major media). Why does Beno have to go hunt minerals instead of playing with his friends? Why are adults so addicted to phones and work instead of playing with their kids? Why don't Zoe's parents work with Beno's parents to solve their problems? And why don't they share the natural and material wealth if there is enough for everyone?

'We are sorry for the inconvenience, but this is a revolution'

Mainstream economic thinking, some will say, can answer all my children's questions. It can answer with sophisticated mathematical models that confirm that we live in the best version of the world that is possible. Of course, they will say, there is room for improvement. But overall we are on the right track. 'We don't say so, science and numbers do'. However, economic science is not and cannot be objective. It has always been subjective and political.

Why do you reckon we used to call economic science 'political economy' instead of 'economics' which is the norm today? Why evoke physics and feign objectivity? Economics is now like physics. The numbers tell us what needs to be done beyond ideologies and fixations. That might be the case in physics (at least as far as we currently understand it), but in economics the numbers tell the story you want them to. 'Get politics out of economics', they tell us. Let's depoliticise it.

Beno's home, the Democratic Republic of the Congo (DRC), is rich in minerals. Therefore, according to mainstream economic thinking, the comparative advantage for Beno and his compatriots is the mining of precious minerals (copper, cobalt, lithium, tantalum, etc.). The DRC needs to specialise in mining and the advanced industrialised states need to specialise in using what Beno and his people mine. From mining mineral wealth to mining football players.

The average British, Spanish, or German player present at the 2022 Qatar World Cup has spent almost his entire career in his home country. But for Senegalese, Ghanaian, Moroccan, and Cameroonian players, the picture is the exact opposite. European clubs have the money to maintain their talent and import too. African football fans like to watch the top European leagues on TV because of the considerable number of African players featured. Instead of watching them play in their weak national leagues, they watch them in European stadiums while African stadiums are empty.

The poorest countries are trapped in a vicious cycle that prevents them from developing the infrastructure that would retain players and build better football. 'In the long run, this means that African football is not developing itself anymore. It's like raw materials', says Gerard Akindes, a professor of sports management at Hamad Bin Khalifa University. 'You export it, you make some money, and it comes back with added value for you to consume. It's like exporting oil and then buying rubber afterwards'.

The dominant system that determines the economy also determines football. Inequalities in the economy are reproduced as well. 'Let the free market do its job and a society of abundance awaits you round the corner', they tell us. Yet experience shows the opposite. The gap between rich and poor is widening and environmental disaster is here. The surpluses of the rich are based on the deficits of the poor. Some states have specialised in being poor and others in being rich.

Rich states have created their wealth not only through innovation and the hard work of their citizens. They became rich after years of exploiting people and nature (hint: colonialism). Then, having first protected their home economies to make them strong and competitive, they threw poor countries onto the free market wolves. In the name of 'freedom' and 'democracy', of course.

In the early 1990s, with the Soviet Union dissolved and China undergoing massive reforms, the World Trade Organization along with the World Economic Forum were geared to be in charge of the global economy for many years to come. On New Year's Day 1994, the Mexican government signed the North American Free Trade Agreement (NAFTA) with the US and Canada. This allowed them to have free economic activity in Mexico. That is, everything that had somehow escaped the claws of colonialism over the past centuries would now be primed for the taking.

Preparations for the signing of the Agreement included the annulment of Article 27 of the Mexican Constitution, a key achievement of the 1910–1919 Revolution. Under Article 27, in a country where large parts of the population are Indigenous, communal lands were prohibited from being privatised. However, the article was not in keeping with the spirit of the North American Free Trade Agreement. Rightfully, Indigenous rural populations feared they would lose their communal lands. They also feared that cheaper products from the US and Canada would compete with their own local products.

On the same New Year's Day, the Zapatista Army of National Liberation (EZLN) rose up in Chiapas. The Zapatistas viewed the impending Free Trade Agreement as a 'death sentence' for the future of Indigenous peoples. They joined with others in solidarity and began their struggle for equality, freedom, and dignity through the now-autonomous Chiapas. They declared war against the Mexican state and seized land and government buildings. They clashed with the Mexican army and suffered many casualties in the process. In their first press release, from the jungle of Lacandon in Chiapas, they wrote 'But today we say – enough is enough!' (¡ya basta!). Since 1994, in Chiapas, women and men have been building self-managed communities through collective action. Zapatistas are resisting and creating another world. They have inspired millions worldwide.

On 8 July 1996, Subcomandante Marcos, a leading Zapatista figure, sent a letter to Eduardo Galeano (1940–2015) – a Uruguayan writer and journalist whose work inspired this book. Galeano was perhaps the first to eloquently highlight the political dimension of football. Marcos wrote to Galeano about Olivio, a child of the Tojolabal tribe. Marcos told Galeano that children in Chiapas do not often live past the age of 5. The mortality rate is twice that for non-Indigenous residents of Mexico.

And yet, Olivio was full of life, chasing a ball a Zapatista leader had kicked away. Olivio raced for the ball through mud and dung and ran past all defenders in front of him – a tree and two kids who were more apprehensive of the mud. Marcos watched the tiny footballer gear up for a score. Olivio suddenly stopped dribbling when he spotted a bird near him. He dropped the ball for a gun so he could hunt it. If Olivio caught the bird, he could feed his family. In Chiapas, people wear military uniforms today, so that tomorrow their children will wear football uniforms, wrote Markos. It is high time we pushed Olivio's ball into the net.

15
The Cruyff turn

A certain method of providing kinetic energy to another ball, the golf ball, was patented by lawyer Dale Miller in 1996 in the US. Miller's technique describes striking the ball while holding the club with your right hand only while using your left hand to support the right. According to Miller's patent, the patented putt offers enhanced control of direction and speed. Until 2016, when the patent expired, using this technique required Miller's explicit permission.

Getting back to football, French striker Yves Mariot, who played for several top teams in the 1970s, made the 'Roulette', '360', or 'Marseille turn' move internationally famous. Later, players like Maradona or Zidane would refine and popularise it further. So, imagine if one of them had patented it. Or if Johan Cruyff had patented the iconic sharp dribble he made in the 24th minute of the Netherlands' match against Sweden in the 1974 World Cup. Because of its simplicity, beauty, and effectiveness, this dribble is still one of the most popular in football history. The fact that it has gone down in history as the 'Cruyff turn' does not, of course, mean that Cruyff was the first to perform it. Its origins are unknown. However, it was certainly the flying Dutchman who made it famous. Imagine how poor the sport would be if players patented their signature moves. Prevented others from repeating, enriching, and ingraining them in collective memory.

'Could you patent the sun?'

Strict intellectual property rights is a key pillar of the system that defines our lives: capitalism. Knowledge is inherently free, and when it is shared it becomes more valuable. More people thus have access to knowledge and the experts among them can improve it. Patents commodify knowledge of any kind. They make it scarce when it is born free. This artificial scarcity is a prerequisite for profit. Capitalism bottles knowledge. Unequal access to knowledge creates further inequalities. During the COVID-19 pandemic, these inequalities were starkly displayed with the patented vaccines against the virus.

During the 1920s, three Canadian researchers developed insulin to treat diabetes. At the time, the prevailing view was that scientists were to create new knowledge and share it with humanity. So, they sold the patent to the University of Toronto for a dollar. Before the discovery of insulin, the lives of people with diabetes were short. Now hundreds of millions of diabetics lead full lives.

A few years later, Dr Jonas Salk developed the polio vaccine. At that time, the average number of polio victims in the US alone was about 45,000. With Salk's vaccine, the number would drop below 1000 victims. In 1955, when asked by a journalist about who owned the patent on the vaccine he had invented, Salk replied, 'The people, I would say. There is no patent. Could you patent the sun?'

Why is it, then, that COVID-19 vaccines are owned by private pharmaceutical companies and not by the people? We offer most of the production of drugs and vaccines to the private sector, despite huge public investment and public participation in research funding. Government policy has encouraged universities to patent publicly funded medical research and then transfer that knowledge to pharmaceutical companies for product development, with no strings attached. Companies, after conducting clinical trials to show the safety and efficacy of the drug or vaccine, often with further public funding, become the sole owners of the product and the research data. And because companies compete for market share, they keep their methods and research results secret so that other companies cannot copy or develop them further.

Since pharmaceutical companies are accountable to shareholders and financial markets alone, they seek to maximise profit by charging unaffordable prices for their drugs and vaccines, especially in rich countries, rather than producing and pricing them so that they are available to all. So, despite large public investments in research, taxpayers still have to pay for access to its results. For individuals and countries that cannot afford them, access remains elusive. The World Health Organization estimates that 2 billion people lack access to essential medicines, excluding them from the benefits of advances in modern science.

It need not be this way: When knowledge is freely shared, we can build on each other's ideas and creativity. We can work together to make the best possible treatments to improve the lives of people everywhere. Without patents and monopolies, knowledge and technologies can be shared openly, allowing companies and countries everywhere to produce pharmaceutical treatments. So instead of selling medicines as products for profit, medicines should be 'public goods' or 'global health commons' – available and accessible to all. Taking all public investment into account, governments must stop handing over all property rights to private companies. Rather, they need to promote a culture of exchange and cooperation. We need a global commons of knowledge, i.e. an immaterial commons adhering to the same principles of openness and communal stewardship as the material ones.

The issue of patents and strict intellectual property has, seemingly, nothing to do with football. For now at least. It may become directly relevant as technology enters and affects football. However, it does link directly to the inequalities that we, through football, wish to communicate and address. As I will attempt to illustrate, it is all connected and all can change. Change can be ignited in the most unexpected of places. – from the fringes of society, or from the edge of the pitch. When the opponent thinks they are in complete control of the game, suddenly a ball appears, out of nowhere, over their head and under their feet.

16
So can the world change through football?

The poor are staggeringly more numerous than the rich; the ruled are overwhelmingly more abundant than the rulers; there are startlingly more men in positions of power than there are women. And all this amid a climate catastrophe that affects primarily the weakest and most vulnerable. Poor people, women, children, and animals. In time though, those in power will be affected too. There is no escaping this predicament.

Many believe that this is just how things are. That inequalities and oppression are natural phenomena. That we live in the best possible version of the world. 'Be thankful for what you have. Those who excel may progress. Believe in your dreams and if you don't give up you will eventually succeed', say the prophets and apologists of the dominant system. 'History is over', they proclaim. But the struggle ends with the final whistle. And this has yet to be heard. We're behind in the score, but there's still a chance.

Is there anything to stand against the insatiable thirst for increasingly material wealth? As sermons on perpetual economic growth have led to a profound environmental crisis, is there a viable alternative that recognises natural limits? Is there another way of organising our society that promotes cooperation and solidarity over competition and exploitation? And if there is, how can a ball help us bring that change about?

Ursula Le Guin (1929–2018) created alternative worlds where her inhabitants could live free and in harmony with nature. In 2014 she was awarded the National Book Foundation Medal for Distinguished Contribution to American Letters. Upon receiving the medal, Le Guin stated: 'We live in capitalism, its power seems inescapable – but then, so did the divine right of kings. Any human power can be resisted and changed by human beings. Resistance and change often begin in art. Very often in our art, the art of words'.

What we experience as present is not static, not permanent. It is a dynamic process. It is the product of constant probing and change. Cooperation coexists with competition. Pretty much like a football match. The world is constantly changing. Change is the result of the conflict between the past and the future we imagine and desire. Some want a future that promotes competition and the maximisation of monetary gain. Others want a future that is more collaborative and inclusive. Some come from a past of exploitation and concentration of power, others from a past of oppression and struggle for autonomy.

Le Guin's work shows us that one of the most powerful tools at our disposal is imagination. To change the world we must be able to imagine alternatives. We cannot understand injustice unless we imagine justice. We cannot understand exploitation if we do not imagine solidarity. We cannot understand oppression if we do not imagine freedom. We have to imagine where we wish to go. Our next step and the step after that. With and without a ball.

However, it is important to have a solid understanding of current reality. To be able to empathise with others (not just people) in this world. To be cognisant of our position in space and the position of our teammates. Many modern football stars, comfortable in their bubble, seem indifferent to the tragedy of our times. Therefore, the first step is to acknowledge and bring attention to the ills of our reality. Football can make the fight against injustice, inequality, and climate catastrophe its supreme task.

In dark times, hope is a lifeboat, drifting away from the sinking ship. Floating towards an alternative future and a new vision; a journey that will nurture us. Football can create regenerative moments, and glimpses into another world: a world of cooperation, solidarity, and commitment to the simple things that make people truly content. In one of Le Guin's best books, *The Dispossessed*, protagonist Shevek says, while addressing a crowd during a demonstration, 'You cannot buy the Revolution. You cannot make the Revolution. You can only be the Revolution'. But how can we become the revolution using a ball?

PART III
How to change the world through football

17
The turn of the century

When snow falls on a mountain peak, one day it shall melt away and water springs will form. Tiny streams will trickle down the slopes, coalescing to form ever bigger rivers. All rushing rivers start from unassuming streams.

So many of the biggest changes in the world have started quietly, far away from where its biggest effect will be felt – on the fringes of society, on the edge of the field, where the opponent does not expect the oncoming move forward. A shift in play that does not foreshadow its aim can be the start of the most beautiful goal in a match or even a whole season. A goal to spark the turn of the century.

> 'I don't think I should stand up'

On a rainy day in 1943, in Montgomery, Alabama, Black woman Rosa Parks (1913-2005) boards a bus. She pays her fare and occupies an empty seat. The white driver tells her to get off and get back on the bus through the back door. Like she is supposed to. Parks gets off and before she has the chance to board again, the bus speeds off. Parks waits for the next bus in the rain.

Twelve years later, on a winter afternoon in 1955, Parks boards another bus. She pays her fare and sits in an empty seat in the front row of the back seats. The spot where Black people were required to sit. The first four rows of buses in Montgomery were reserved for white people. Black people rows were usually in the back of the bus. A Black person could sit in the middle rows until the white seats were filled. If white passengers needed more seats, then Black passengers would move to the back. If there were no available seats, they had to stand. If there was no room for that either, they were required to get off the bus. Meanwhile, the vast majority of people using buses in Montgomery were Black.

Parks's seat was directly behind the white passengers' seats. As the bus rolled on, it gradually filled up. The white driver noticed some white passengers standing. So the driver demanded that Parks and three other Black passengers stand up so the white passengers could sit. Three stand up. Parks, however, did not. 'Why don't you stand up?' the driver asks her. 'I don't think I should stand up', Parks replies. The driver then calls the police, who arrest Parks. It was the same driver who had left her in the rain twelve years earlier.

Parks's resistance and subsequent arrest led to a widespread boycott of buses and inspired thousands of people in the US. Among them was the pastor of a small town church. Martin Luther King (1929–1968) who would, as a human rights activist, go on to lead an all-American movement to eliminate racial discrimination. Both Parks's and King's portraits now adorn a wall in the White House. Both were streams in a small town in the American South that joined with other streams to form a torrent. Every tiny action can be part of cataclysmic change. We have seen that everything – goals, music, culture, science – is created in common and therefore so is social change.

Parks' story is similar, and perhaps an inspiration, to women in Iran who have been banned from football grounds since 1981. In 2004, at a friendly match in Tehran between Iran and Germany, Iranian women clashed with police who prevented them from entering the stadium. This clash created a movement, with people protesting by wearing white headscarves.

The movement emboldened by Parks's action and the white headscarves in Iran are movements of resistance. Resistance against all kinds of oppression perpetrated by those in power and those aiming to consolidate their privileges. Change, however, needs resistance and creation at the same time in order to imagine, experiment, and co-create new structures that will not allow a regression to a society Parks helped change and one that Iranian women are still fighting against. Movements against racial and gender discrimination have come a long way. They have created new structures: laws, changes in the education system, and new cultural artefacts. Much more work needs to be done.

In this third and final part of this book, we will witness attempts to resist the oppressing old and attempts to create the liberating new. These efforts are on and off the pitch. Some come from the past. Others from a potential future we can and must build together. With a football in front of us. So let's strive for the turn of the century.

18
Drivers should drive and footballers should kick the ball

FIA (Fédération Internationale de l'Automobile) is the International Automobile Federation that represents the interests of motoring organisations and motor car users. FIFA is, as is well known, the organisation that governs football worldwide – the Vatican of the football world if you will. What do FIA and FIFA have in common? They both discourage (or sometimes prohibit) the 'politicisation' of the sports they govern. From 1 January 2023, the FIA prohibited Formula 1 drivers from making public statements and interventions of any political, religious, or social nature without first obtaining its formal written approval. Both FIFA's stance at the Qatar World Cup and the FIA's regulation constitute an authoritarian shift in sports and society. 'Don't upset our sponsors and their oil money. Don't disturb the speculation of federations. Humanitarians should exit the building. The answer to any question is this: money!'

'I can't live on an island that is encircled by poverty'

In March 2020, Black woman Breonna Taylor was fatally shot by seven police officers in Louisville, Kentucky. The officers had forcibly entered her home following a mistaken suspicion of drug trafficking. Taylor was innocent. A few days later, at the Tuscany Grand Prix, a seven-time champion and first

Black driver in Formula 1 history, Lewis Hamilton, wears a T-shirt with the message 'Arrest the cops who killed Breonna Taylor'. A year later, Sebastian Vettel, another Formula 1 champion, wears a rainbow-coloured T-shirt at the starting ceremony of the Hungarian Grand Prix. The shirt features the message 'Same Love', in support of LGBTQ+ rights and against the Hungarian ultra-conservative government's legislative actions. In both cases, the FIA required drivers to wear only their team's clothing and so Vettel was reprimanded.

And yet, neither was deterred. In the last three Grand Prix of 2021 (Qatar, Saudi Arabia, and Abu Dhabi) Hamilton wore a rainbow-coloured helmet. All three countries have punitive laws for members of the LGBTQ+ community. 'It's important for me to represent this community here because I know there are some situations that can't be imperfect and need to be highlighted', Hamilton stated.

Vettel was unfettered too. In December 2021, he organised a women's go-kart race in Saudi Arabia in support of gender equality. In 2022, during several Grand Prix, the German driver used his helmet and T-shirts to promote the need to tackle the climate crisis. Shortly after, Mercedes F1 director Toto Wolff said such initiatives 'can trigger change because things can no longer be hidden'.

FIA's core tenet is purported neutrality. This is reminiscent of FIFA and the events at the 2022 World Cup held in Qatar. According to a 2021 report by Amnesty International, workers in Qatar 'face labour abuses' and homosexuality is still a criminal offence. Several World Cup participants protested. Some with public statements, others wearing the rainbow-coloured 'One Love' armband. Players of the German national team, in their team photo before the kick-off of their first World Cup match, covered their mouths. 'We wanted to convey the message that FIFA is silencing us', coach Hansi Flick stated.

FIFA quickly reacted and threatened the team with sanctions. They demanded everyone stay 'committed to football' and leave politics out of it. 'Footballers are for kicking the ball and drivers are for driving cars'. However, there is no such thing as politically neutral. Everything is politics. FIFA's and FIA's interventions against politicking are deeply political. They are an attempt to maintain incumbent structures that shower them with money and power. Athletes are, however, human beings, and human being are political animals. Celebrity athletes have massive platforms from which to speak out from, giving them the audiences and power that oppressed people could only ever dream of.

The Brazilian Grand Prix is held at Interlagos in São Paulo. Some curious drivers of Formula 1's ultra-modern cars slow down just before the last corner of the track. They're not seeking to reduce their carbon emissions. They slow down to peek, outside the walls, at the favelas. Inside the walls, expensive cars race, people cheer, and adrenaline is rushing. Millions of dollars change hands and most of it is collected in a few white men's pockets. Outside the walls, the poor live in squalor … Ayrton Senna (1960–1994), a star Formula 1 driver, was born into a wealthy Brazilian family. Three decades ago, gazing out the window of his expensive car he famously mused: 'Wealthy men can't live on an island that is encircled by poverty. We all breathe the same air. We must give a chance to everyone, at least a basic chance'.

19
Democracy in football, democracy in society

Brazilian footballer Socrates breathed the same air as Senna. During the time Senna was transitioning from kart racing to Formula 1 cars, Socrates, along with his team, was transitioning from resistance to creation. They initiated an experiment with the Corinthians that would make football history – the Corinthian Republic (Democracia Corinthiana). The Corinthians were founded in 1910 by five immigrant railway workers in São Paulo, at a time when football was a sport reserved for the elite.

However, 54 years later, when the Corinthians were already one of the most successful clubs in Brazil, the country's army overthrew the democratically elected socialist president João Goulart. The coup brought a military dictatorship to power that lasted for 25 years. All in accordance with the interests of the US government. Socrates was not politicised before he joined the Corinthians in 1978. He had an apolitical, if not friendly, attitude towards the regime. He preferred a carefree, bohemian life – which defined him to the very end. However, his political views would change radically with his transfer to the Corinthians.

'Win or lose, but always with democracy'

Socrates met several kindred spirits in the Corinthians with whom he would later create the Corinthian Republic. He met

Walter Casagrande, an unflappable 19-year-old striker with iconic curly hair. He also met the politically minded Afro-Brazilian Wladimir Rodrigues, a defender and prominent figure in the team's history. It was his meeting with a sociologist, Adilson Monteiro Alves, that was the catalyst. Alves, while having no experience as a football manager, was to take over the reins of the team by the decision of the club's president, Waldemar Pires. Under Alves, Socrates would drink a lot of beer and smoke a lot of cigarettes in the years to come. The Corinthian Republic would slowly emerge in 1981.

Since the late 1970s, the country embarked on a process of democratisation, albeit at a glacial pace. Authoritarianism held fast. What could the Corinthians do about it? 'What were we going to do? No idea', says Alves in the documentary *Football Rebels*, hosted by Eric Cantona. He adds: 'But I knew what we couldn't. I knew we couldn't continue living like we were. We had to end authoritarianism. We had to break with conservatism. So what did we do? We started defining things together'.

So a meeting was held with the whole team. This meeting was meant to last only a few minutes. Socrates took the floor and proclaimed they should all decide on their fates together. Minutes turned into hours. The meeting was interminable. Some grew tired. Others got bored and left. Others were simply indifferent. But the enthusiastic few stayed and the conversation went on. 'We worked out as a group how we should proceed', says Alves. 'We started discussing things and it created a really convivial atmosphere. Each of us started giving his opinion and expressing his feelings', Socrates stresses in a later interview, when returning to the subject as a veteran.

In 1982 the players presented a new management model. 'The club wasn't just about the players. The whole group, masseurs, stewards, doctors, trainers, coaches, everyone,

everyone had a vote. And the majority would win'. Wladimir explains in *Football Rebels*. All this in the midst of a military dictatorship. For Wladimir, it all started when Kazagrade didn't want to join the team on a tour in Japan. He was madly in love and wished to stay with his then-partner. The whole team agreed to vote. All of them. And they decided that Casagrande should stay. And so he did. From then on, everyone would vote for everything. All would be up for discussion. Transfers, bonuses, the in-game system. 'They would even vote on when the bus would stop for a toilet break', journalist Juca Kfouri tells *Football Rebels*.

They also debated philosophy, politics, and art. They held group therapy sessions. They invited painters, architects, filmmakers, and other artists for discussions. Turns out, deep discussions formed excellent training sessions if their match statistics are any indication. For the first time since the 1950s, the Corinthians won two straight championships in 1982 and 1983. The word Corinthians on the back of their jerseys resembled the Coca-Cola logo. Above, was the word 'Republic' with blood splattered around it. Underneath was each player's number.

After almost 20 years, when free elections were held in Brazil, the Corinthian Republic would not sit idly by. Many Brazilians had forgotten what it was like to vote, others feared reprisals from the regime if they did, and the younger generation never had the opportunity to. To encourage people to vote, the Corinthians printed the slogan 'On the 15th [of the month] you vote' (DIA 15 VOTE) on their jerseys. The team played five matches before the elections wearing these jerseys.

The Corinthians created a movement. 'You take several unhappy couples. And in with them you put a really happy couple, who are in love. It contaminates the whole group.

That's how it was with us', Socrates says. According to Brazil's three-time elected president Lula, 'You're Corinthians when you're the champion, Corinthians when you lose, Corinthians when you draw, Corinthians when you win'. At the same time, many journalists, politicians, and businessmen were against this movement. They viewed it as anarchist or communist. The Corinthian Republic was not just about football. When Corinthian players were asked about the game, they often changed the subject and talked about the need for more public hospitals and schools. 'Football is a laboratory of how life should be', Cantona says, staring at the *Football Rebels* camera.

On 14 December 1983, during the finals, a banner was raised in the crowded stands of the Morumbi Stadium. The banner, which would make history, read: 'Win or lose, but always with democracy' (*Ganhar ou perder, mas sempre com democracia*). Comradeship, solidarity, dignity, and courage were ideals the Corinthian Republic brought to football and Brazilian society. Its purpose was to strengthen the movement for democratic elections; to politicise the world through football.

In 1984, Socrates spoke in front of 1.5 million people at a rally for democratic elections in São Paulo. He said that if Congress would not restore democracy to the country, he would continue his career in Italy. Congress did not restore democracy and Socrates left for ACF Fiorentina in Florence, where he played for one season. That was the end of the Corinthian Republic. Shortly afterwards the dictatorship would fall.

When Socrates was in Italy he said that instead of luxury cars and mansions, he was interested in books. A journalist asked him which footballer of the time he appreciated more, Inter's Mazzola or Milan's Rivera. Socrates replied: 'I don't know them. I am here to read Gramsci [Italian Marxist philosopher] in its original language and to study the history of the labour movement'.

In 1983, Socrates proclaimed he would like to die on a Sunday with the Corinthians crowned champions. And so he did. On Sunday, 4 December 2011, the day the Corinthians won the championship, Socrates died. The stadium was packed to capacity. A moment of silence was declared in honour of their former captain. The players of Corinthians and Palmeiras formed a circle before the start of the match. The fans raised their fists. The Corinthians joined them. A very "happy sad day", as Socrates might have put it.

In the decades that followed, the Corinthian Republic would inspire a movement of politicisation in football. Self-managed football clubs would pop up across the globe. These clubs were and are a response to commercialised football. An attempt to create a utopia in the now. The self-organised groups promote ideas and values such as equality, solidarity, fair play, anti-fascism, anti-racism, and anti-sexism. They are usually amateur teams and refrain from sponsorships and advertising. Their operating costs are covered by self-financing of the athletes and the wider community through events and festivals. Decision-making is done through direct democratic processes in which all who follow the team, in any capacity, are usually involved.

In professional football, a prominent case of a club imbued with some of the Corinthian Republic ideas is the German FC St Pauli. The club was founded in 1910 in Hamburg. But it was in the mid-1980s, when the Corinthian Republic was coming full circle, that St Pauli began building its (political) legend. The team played primarily in the German second division (2. Bundesliga). In 1981, the average attendance did not exceed 1600. In the late 1990s, the 20,000-seat stadium was suffocatingly full. Its reputation is not linked to the football it plays but to the culture of its fans. The club is aligned with the poor and marginalised. On and off the pitch, it promotes values such as solidarity, anti-fascism, anti-racism, and anti-sexism. St Pauli was the first club in Germany, the country that gave birth to Nazism, to ban any fascist/Nazi symbol from its stadium.

It would be naive and, potentially, dangerous to romanticise these efforts. All these projects have faced and still face financial, organisational, and moral problems and deadlocks. Let us cast away the rose-tinted glasses. When everything around us is a far cry from the world we wish to create, we ought to have one foot here and one foot there. One needs patience, courage, empathy, and several lessons in balance. We are moving contradictions.

In a previous chapter, I wrote about the problems of modern technologies. And yet, I wrote this book on a high-end laptop and I shudder to think about the process it went through before it reached my hands. How much child labour, most likely under inhumane conditions, and how much pollution has this laptop caused? I wrote before and will reiterate here about the need for the free sharing of ideas and knowledge. You are probably reading this in a book you paid money for. We are moving contradictions, staggering along.

But there are moments when history accelerates. It's hard to tell when. Perhaps we are experiencing such an acceleration right now. Sometimes it's only after the game is over that we realise how momentous it was.

20
Perhaps the greatest match of all time

A match for the ages took place in the 1970s in Munich. The German national team of philosophers and the Greek national team of philosophers were pitted against each other. I am referring to the 'International Philosophy' match. A legendary Monty Python sketch that was first broadcast on West German television in 1972.

Educated in Oxbridge (Oxford and Cambridge Universities) the Monty Python comedy troupe often made philosophical references in their sketches. There's even a word in the Oxford dictionary to describe Python's surreal yet grounded and liberating humour: 'Pythonesque'. Terry Jones, a member of Python, had expressed his frustration with the existence of such a term since their original goal was to create something new and difficult to categorise. 'That "Pythonesque" is now an adjective ... means we failed utterly', he told the *New York Times* in 2009. No matter how Jones felt about it, Python succeeded in radically changing comedy and satire. The Match of the Philosophers is one of my favourite works of art.

The forecasts spoke of a close match. How could it not be? Germany, under the direction of Martin Luther, fielded Leibniz, Kant, Schopenhauer, Schelling, Beckenbauer (the footballer who is not a philosopher, or is he?), Jaspers, Schlegel, Wittgenstein, Nietzsche, Heidegger, and team captain Hegel. On the other side, Greece lined up Plato, Epictetus, Aristotle, Sophocles, Empedocles, Plotinus, Epicurus, Heraclitus, Democritus, Archimedes, and captain Socrates. The referee of the game was Confucius, who held an hourglass instead of a watch, and his assistants were Augustine of Hippo and Thomas Aquinas.

The philosophers took to the field early, warmed up, and assumed their positions, waiting for Confucius's whistle. The Greeks were dressed in chlamys (ancient Greek cloaks). The Germans in Victorian jackets, riding pants, high hats, and other period clothing. Only Beckenbauer was dressed in the uniform of Bayern Munich. As soon as the opening whistle blew, the philosophers started walking in deep contemplation. All except Beckenbauer who, as the only professional footballer, found it difficult to understand what was happening. In the first half, Nietzsche was carded for disrespecting referee Confucius by telling him he had no free will.

In the second half, the deep reflections and laborious contemplation continued. The score was stuck at zero for both teams. Just before the end, Martin Luther signalled Marx to warm-up. Marx replaced Wittgenstein and after a tremendous sprint without the ball, he too fell into deep walking reflection. A minute before the end of the game, Archimedes screamed out: 'Eureka!'. Then he kicked the ball, which had remained static since the start of the match, and the Greek team burst into the offence. The German team watched, distracted, as the Greeks deftly switched the ball and captain Socrates scored with a header in the last minute.

The Germans protested strongly to the referee. Hegel informed him that reality is just an *a priori* appendix of non-naturalistic morality. Kant pointed out that the goal exists ontologically only in the imagination. While Marx claimed that the goal was offside. Was Marx right? The video replay showed that Socrates was indeed offside. Nevertheless, in the absence of VAR, the goal stood. Football Marx was clearly right. But what about the political Marx? Why does it matter if he was right or what exactly he was right about?

'Things are more complicated'

Karl Marx (1818–1883) was a German philosopher, journalist, economist, and revolutionary socialist. He studied law and philosophy at the universities of Bonn and Berlin. Marx was one of the most influential people in human history – at least in the last 200 years. His work has both fierce supporters and ardent detractors. Yet few of them have read it and even fewer have understood it.

Many have a vague or superficial understanding of Marx's prediction that capitalism will inevitably be replaced by communism. In the thousands of pages of his work, there are but a few references to what communism will look like. Marx was primarily a student of capitalism, recognising the dynamics of the system and its inherent weaknesses. He offered no blueprint for transitioning to socialism or communism. However, he did offer one of the most thorough analyses of the nature of the incumbent socioeconomic system since the Industrial Revolution.

He was wrong on a few points though. For example, we don't just have two warring social classes – the rich and the workers – as Marx believed. Things are more complicated. And of course, capitalism hasn't collapsed (yet). Perhaps one of the reasons it didn't collapse was that some people actually read Marx. So, they were able to deal, however ephemerally, with some of its contradictions. The lives of many improved while, as we have seen in previous chapters, the lives of others, along with natural ecosystems, deteriorated. One instance of accounting for Marx's ideas is the creation of the 'welfare state' with its system of progressive income taxation and public access to health and education. Another is Henry Ford's doubling of workers' wages in 1914 so that workers could buy the Ford car they produced.

However, Marx predicted with impressive accuracy, given that he wrote in the mid-nineteenth century, various aspects of modern capitalism. He explained that the nature of capitalism is inherently chaotic and prone to crises, such as the global financial crisis of 1929 or that of 2008. He argued that the unquenchable thirst for profit would lead capitalists to ever-increasing automation of production using new machines, producing more and more goods. At the same time, the real wages of workers would decline until they could no longer buy the products they created. Moreover, environmental destruction would be a consequence of the endless pursuit of profit. Like over-consumption, globalisation, and the creation of monopolies (big company predators devouring the small fry) were phenomena that Marx foresaw two centuries ago. He was no prophet, but he deeply understood how the capitalist system works.

The fifth chapter (in the second part of this book, Chapter 11) on the tragedy of our times is based on Marx's work. I turn to Marx, as American economist Robert Heilbroner would say, not because he is infallible, but because he is inevitable. We cannot understand the nature of modern football, its problems, and its potential for change unless we understand the dominant framework (capitalism for those who haven't got it yet) within which it was created and still evolves.

One of Marx's most important contributions is his analysis of how human history is changing. In short, to survive we have to work. We have to find food, water, shelter, and a relatively safe habitat. Only then can we further develop the sciences, arts, philosophy, and more. Human labour, then, is at the centre of the evolution of human history. From the earliest hunter-gatherer communities to the technologically complex societies of today, we have had to work together to survive. So we invent and use new tools and techniques to help us meet our physical needs more efficiently. From fire and sharp tools to the internet and artificial intelligence, old and new technologies are giving us new possibilities to produce what we need and desire.

While we work and produce, we develop connections with each other. If we experience competition daily at work, we tend to internalise it. It shapes us and defines our daily lives. We want more money, a faster car, a house with a big pool, and more World Cups. If our work is mechanised, that is, if we are a cog in a mega-machine, we are often not satisfied with our work. We get bored. Our self-esteem decreases. We lose meaning. We lose our sense of self. Simply put, Marx argues that the way we produce largely determines the way we think, enjoy ourselves, raise our children, fall in love, and play or watch football.

Marx sees economic conditions as the basis of society. Laws, education, art, and other facets of intellectual and social life are the tip of the iceberg. The economy is what gives rise to and determines everything else. Does the chicken make the egg or does the egg make the chicken? Marx tells us that it is mainly the chicken (i.e. the economy) that makes the egg (i.e. everything else). In other words, how we make our living largely determines our thinking and behavioural patterns. I'm not sure if that's the case (if I thought ideological debate is futile I wouldn't be writing this book). Marx was simultaneously right and not right. Perhaps as much as the chicken makes the egg, the egg also makes the chicken. But that is of little import.

Marx allows for the contingency that some changes in the realm of ideas may affect and shape the base, i.e. the 'real' economy. As we saw Le Guin say, 'resistance and change often begin in art', i.e. art is the very tip of Marx's iceberg. Le Guin informs us that imagination is perhaps the most powerful tool for social change. To change our reality we need to imagine alternatives. Then we can start building them, making mistakes, learning, and moving forward.

Football is defined by the context within which it develops and evolves. No doubt modern capitalist values – competition, showmanship, maximisation of monetary gains, victory as an end in itself, the scorer being the most important player – have a profound effect on it. We have seen, in previous chapters, moments of resistance from the world of sports against these capitalist values. There are, of course, many more such moments. Documentaries (for example, *Rebel Stories* I referred to earlier) and hundreds of books have documented such stories. We have also seen how the Corinthian Republic and other self-organised groups have tried, and are striving still, to prefigure another world. They are glimpses into an alternative organisation and production system for the art of football. Moments of resistance and creation do exist in football.

Marx and Le Guin would have agreed that these moments of creative change (in football) can be strengthened if they are interwoven with similar creative changes in the economy as a whole. And vice versa. A new economy can shape a new football, on and off the pitch, and a new football can shape a new economy. But is there a new economy? A new system. An existent paradigm that can challenge and overcome capitalism? It is now the time to tell you about the thing I have been holding out on so far. About an emerging productive phenomenon that I have been studying for the past 15 years of my life. My response to the above question is: Yes, there sure is.

21
Another world is here

Imagine an open pasture where farmers graze their cows. The farmers' motivation is to fatten their animals up as much as possible. We soon reach a point where the shared resource, the pasture, is destroyed by over-exploitation. This is the story employed by American environmentalist Garrett Hardin (1915–2003) in one of the most widely read scientific articles of all time. Published in 1968 in the journal *Science*, he called the over-exploitation of common pastures 'a tragedy of the commons'. This story was and still is used by many scientists, politicians, journalists, and even influencers to demonstrate the need for the privatisation of public assets or at least for state oversight.

And since, as the collapse of the Soviet Union illustrated, state control does not work very well, many argue that privatisation is the only way. 'There is no alternative', they say. The tragedy of the commons is a flag in the hands of free market zealots and privatisers everywhere. 'Privatisation or barbarism!' they shout with one hand raised and the other lining their pockets. Particularly in South American countries, the tragedy of the commons has been a battering ram for the elites to hijack the wealth of Indigenous people. Such a prospect caused the Indigenous peoples in Chiapas, as we saw in a previous chapter, to rise up when their communal lands were threatened.

In truth, the pasture in Hardin's story is not actually a commons, but an open space with no regulatory framework and no communication amongst shepherds. Each shepherd looks out for their own. The Indigenous people of Chiapas, however, coordinated, and rebelled. People talk and, when they do so effectively, they may congregate and cooperate. They may protect and fortify their commons. And they may create new commons.

In 2009, Elinor Ostrom (1933–2012) became the first woman to receive the Nobel Prize in economics. Ostrom, along with generations of inspiring researchers, highlighted examples of local communities successfully managing their commons without the need for government intervention or privatisation. Hardin himself, in his 80s, revised his story by admitting that it was a 'tragedy of unregulated resources' rather than a 'tragedy of the commons'. It is essentially the 'tragedy of the perfectly free market'.

So what is the commons? It is an economic, social, and political system which harkens back to the earliest human societies. The commons include goods that communities manage according to the rules they have established themselves. Unlike capitalism where the owners are the decision-makers, in the commons it is those who use a resource and/or participate in its production who (co-)decide. Therefore, commons means self-management and autonomy. Deep, grassroots democracy.

Examples of commons abound. They may be natural goods, inherited from previous generations, or created collectively. A shepherd community managing their pasture is one such example. The nomadic communities of Vlachs, found across southern Europe, co-managed their grazing fields to ensure optimal use. This resulted in the conservation and longevity of these ecosystems. Other examples include fishing communities with their self-managed fisheries, community forests, irrigation systems, worker cooperatives (i.e. businesses owned by their employees), self-managed football teams, and many more.

The commons empower people to meet their needs through their own means. They foster responsible thinking. They provide a voice to all, reducing inequalities and oppression. They also provide a genuine connection to nature and fellow human beings. In the commons, different relations of production develop. Relationships are based on cooperation, sharing, and solidarity. Relationships that in a word can be described as 'peer-to-peer'. Peer relationships develop in systems where each person can contribute to the creation and maintenance of a common good while benefiting from it. Such relationships existed in early human communities of foragers.

However, peer relations were radically altered when communities went from small and simplistic to large and complex. It became difficult to make decisions quickly and efficiently when many people were called upon to reach a consensus. The need for central leadership emerged. This gave rise to authoritarian regimes, kings, and parliamentary democracy. The direct democracy of ancient Athens, despite its glaring flaws (the non-participation of slaves and women, for example), was a historical example of commons. Multiple examples of commons can be found throughout human history. But it is the widespread adoption of the internet, after the mid-1990s, that has brought peer-to-peer dynamics back into the spotlight.

'Why the commons need not be another pipe dream'

William Morris (1834–1896) is best known today as a Victorian designer who is perpetually in vogue. You can buy Morris merchandise – from coasters to picture frames to ties and mugs – in the gift shops of every big design museum. And if you Google his name, your screen will erupt in cascades of dense, colourful ornaments. Morris was also a radical thinker, a socialist and, after Karl Marx's death, a leader of the Socialist League. A most relevant aspect of Morris's work today is the framework for a commons-based world of cooperation he sketched in his utopian novel *News from Nowhere* (1890), which has striking applications for the digital age.

In *News from Nowhere*, Morris imagines a world in which human happiness and economic activity coincide. He reminds us that there needs to be a point to labour beyond making ends meet – and there is. Unalienated labour creates happiness for all – consumer and creator; whereas modern capitalism, in contrast, has created a treadmill in which this aspect of work has been lost. Capitalism, he explains, locks the capitalist into a meaningless life, which leads nowhere but the grave.

Morris's utopian society has no government nor a monetary system. Craftwork has made 'wage slavery' obsolete, and parliamentary democracy has given way to new forms of cooperation. The means of production are democratically controlled, and people find pleasure in sharing their interests, goals, and resources. The central character and narrator, William Guest, finds himself in conversation with a young girl, a citizen of Morris's utopian society:

> She disappeared again, and came back with a big-bowled pipe in her hand, carved out of some hard wood very elaborately, and mounted in gold sprinkled with little gems. It was, in short, as pretty, and gay a toy as I had ever seen; something like the best kind of Japanese work, but better.

'Dear me!' said I, when I set eyes on it, 'this is altogether too grand for me or for anybody but the Emperor of the World. Besides, I shall lose it: I always lose my pipes'.

The child seemed rather dashed, and said: 'Don't you like it, neighbour?'

'O yes', I said, 'of course I like it'.

'Well, then, take it', said she, 'and don't trouble about losing it. What will it matter if you do? Somebody is sure to find it, and he will use it, and you can get another'.

When *News from Nowhere* was first published, it had many of the trappings of a classic utopia, including that it appeared practically unattainable. But today, we have different technological potential: the idea and praxis of the commons are more than just a pipe dream. In a sense, the world has caught up with Morris. At the beginning of the twenty-first century, a new world is emerging. Not since Marx identified the manufacturing plants of Manchester as the blueprint for contemporary capitalist society has there been a more profound transformation of the fundamentals of our socioeconomic life. An emerging commons-based paradigm redefines how we (can) produce and relate to each other. And much of this resonates with the little pipe-seller's attitude.

New technologies make it easier for peer-to-peer relationships to scale. Internet-connected computers form networks, allowing people to interact on a global scale. This enables them to collaborate freely and share information and knowledge. However, peer-to-peer does not only refer to the digital world. Peer-to-peer describes the relationships that develop when managing and creating commons. As I mentioned before, peer relationships are as old as humans. Until recently, they could be found in small groups (families, villages, cooperatives). With new technological infrastructures, we are seeing a scaling of peer relationships. And so a new economy, a new way of organising societies is emerging.

In the early 2000s, most people would find a free encyclopaedia, where a worldwide community of people would volunteer content, an absurd proposition. They would find it even more absurd if they were told that this free encyclopaedia would push encyclopaedias backed by giant companies out of the market. And yet, Wikipedia launched in 2001, has put Microsoft's Encarta out of business and forced Britannica to cease its print publication after more than two centuries.

Similarly, few would believe that the world's 500 most powerful computers – forming the backbone of the internet – and most websites would run on software produced in a similar way to Wikipedia. 'From each according to their ability to each according to their needs', to use an old but timely quote. Today the free GNU/Linux software is used by those powerful computers, and the free Apache and nginx software are the most popular software on the web server market.

And if someone were to say that in a similar peer-to-peer fashion, we could produce wind turbines, farm machinery, satellites, and many other things, they would sound fanciful if not bonkers. I was, am, one of those crazies. One of those who believe in the power of human cooperation and the drive to democratise knowledge and technology. This struggle seems, amid much adversity and contradictions, to be paying off: designs, knowledge and software are produced collaboratively and shared globally as commons.

Meanwhile, new, and old manufacturing technologies (from 3D printing and CNC machines to plain soldering and woodworking tools) are increasingly available in shared workshops, enabling communities of people to design a whole host of artefacts like the ones I described above. And they are, to a large extent, made locally. What is 'light' (designs, knowledge, software) becomes global, while what is 'heavy' (machinery) is local and, ideally, shared.

For example, small-scale French farmers require tools matching their practices to make their lives easier. The agribusiness sector rarely bothers with machinery which would not bring in big business. And when they do, maintenance costs are high and farmers are forced to adapt their lifestyle and practices to the machines rather than the other way around. So a community of farmers decided to produce their own machinery through a cooperative called L'Atelier Paysan (peasant workshop). The L'Atelier Paysan community shares its designs and know-how with the world – as a global digital commons. At the same time, a community of small-scale farmers in the US had similar needs. They created a network of farmers called FarmHack with the same goals. The two communities connect, collaborate, and create synergies by contributing to the same digital commons. Such communities have appeared across the globe, bringing in their insight and diverse ways of doing things.

Here is another example, this time from the energy sector: Let's go to the village of Mityal located in southwestern Nepal. The villagers wished to electrify a small community clinic that was difficult to connect to their local grid. So they contacted science and engineering groups working on small-scale wind turbines. Together, based on free designs and jointly generated knowledge, they built a wind turbine locally. Training seminars then took place so that the local community of Mityal could learn how to maintain the infrastructure. With the support of the global network of engineers and activists, Wind Empowerment, such wind turbines have been built in various parts of the world. From South America and sub-Saharan Africa to Nepal and India.

When diverse social groups appropriate a particular technology for their purposes, then social, political, and economic systems can change. An example is the role the printing press played in transforming European society. Similarly, the fast-growing availability of digitisation enables many-to-many communication; think of electronic fora and mailing lists to wikis and Facebook, embattled though it might appear right now. Hence, increasing numbers of humans communicate in ways that were not technically possible. This, in turn, makes massive self-organisation up to a global scale possible. Just as digitisation can work both for emancipation and supervision, and for revolution and its suppression, it also allows for a new mode of production and new social relations outside the market–state nexus.

Even today, it seems inconceivable to many how we can produce such things under much more pleasant conditions than those of the capitalist market. The seeds of a new world can be seen in the examples I have described above. A world based on the sharing of goods and their communal management. That is the commons. It shows that people are not solely motivated to produce by the need to maximise monetary gain. It also shows that competition and a strict patent system are not the quintessence of progress and innovation. Typical capitalist enterprises hire workers, manage them, direct the production process, and sell the goods produced on the market to maximise monetary profit. In contrast, in the examples I have just provided, any person who feels able to contribute participates under a regime of autonomy. Some may be paid, but not necessarily all.

Then why do people contribute to such projects you may wonder. For a multitude of reasons. Let's remember why we play football. Did the pros amongst you start playing for the money? Or for the pleasure of simply doing so? Was it because football, without necessarily being able to explain how and why, provides some meaning in your lives? Our lives. So too people contribute to the commons. Because they learn. Because they communicate. Because they wish to create something useful. First for their own selves and then for their fellow human beings. Also because they can earn an income. But not maximise income. There is a fine line between creating profit and maximising it. The latter leads to the ruthless exploitation of people and natural ecosystems.

William Morris envisioned a future in which humans would be free to create and to 'delight in the life of the world'. Yet, in his opinion, for reasons of scope and human conditioning, violent events – wars, revolutions – would have to precede such freedom. But he might have been wrong about that. Naturally, some of the aforementioned commons-based cases may seem small-scale, bucolic, catering to an Arcadia. A dreamworld for leftie intellectuals. The difference with the commons is that it takes back, through empowerment, what has already been lost, but via a synthesis of old and modern means. It is best to consider these commons-based projects as early pilot projects, with a radical change in our attitudes to production likely around the corner. The danger, where such a path to be fully co-opted by the current (very) dominant context, is obvious, and it must realistically be acknowledged. However, the counterculture is not only here, it is gaining ground so far. Were Morris alive today, he certainly would have recognised its revolutionary potential. What was news from nowhere in 1890 could soon be news from here.

The commons point to the reality of peaceful paths of radical change emerging. Capitalism is, without a doubt, the current dominant system. However, there are other systems inherent in capitalism. The commons have capitalist and post-capitalist aspects. On one hand, many of the projects I have described base their economic viability on alliances with the dominant system. On the other, they break through the core of the system by pointing to new paths. Paths paved with cooperation, solidarity, inclusion, and sharing. Paths that we are invited to carve, explore, experience, and claim through football. How can this be achieved? To answer tentatively, let us fly to Australia, from there to Brazil, and back and forth a couple of times. I think it's worth the trouble for a football of change.

22
The football of change

In the early 1960s, John Kundereri Moriarty (1938–) became the first Aboriginal footballer to play for the Australian national team. Moriarty was quick to realise the social appeal of football. He used the sport to aid the struggle of Aboriginal people, perhaps the oldest civilisation on earth, for equality, freedom, and dignity. At the same time, almost 10,000 kilometres away, another man, the educator and philosopher Paulo Freire (1921–1997), was fighting to improve the lives of oppressed workers in northeastern Brazil. Freire was deeply influenced by the work of Marx. Moriarty through football and Freire through pioneering educational methods sought to free oppressed peoples from their shackles.

Moriarty was born in Borroloola, a small town in Northern Australia. His mother was Aboriginal and his father was Irish. Therefore, according to the British Empire's classification system at the time, Moriarty was listed as 'half-caste'. Thus, when he was 4 years old, the state took Moriarty from his mother. He would not see her again for a decade. Moriarty was a member of the Stolen Generation. Children were forcibly removed from their families from the early twentieth century until the late 1960s.

After passing through several Aboriginal children's homes near Sydney, he ended up in a monastery in Adelaide. There he met other Aboriginal people who years later would fight for Aboriginal rights. It was at this monastery that Moriarty first played football. Soon football became his passion, and his talent was recognised; he was given a pair of football boots and a new goal in life.

Freire was born into a middle-class family in northeastern Brazil. However, following the economic depression of 1929, his family went bankrupt. Freire was forced to face poverty and hunger at a very young age. The family moved to a poor town and Freire was left fatherless in 1934. He did not do well at school: 'I didn't understand anything because of my hunger. I wasn't dumb. It wasn't a lack of interest. My social conditions didn't allow me to have an education. Experience showed me once again the relationship between social class and knowledge', he says.

Eventually, their financial situation improved and Freire studied law and philosophy. Over the next few years, he would work in education, applying on a large scale his pioneering educational methods to eradicate illiteracy among the rural and working class. His work was interrupted by the 1964 coup, when he was imprisoned and then later exiled. In 1968, Freire's most important work, *Pedagogy of the Oppressed* (*Pedagogia do Oprimido*), was published, which influenced, and continues to do so, millions of people even beyond the discipline of education.

Humility, empathy, critical thinking, hope, and courage were key elements of Freire and Moriarty's work. Both, despite obstacles, continue to inspire with their legacy. Both faced adversity which they wished to exorcise from the lives of future generations. In 2022, academics and activists Jorge Knijnik and Jane Hunter published a study on how Freire's critical pedagogy met Moriarty's football philosophy. During the 2014 World Cup, eight teenage Aboriginal players and young coaches from Borroloola visited the host country Brazil. There, with the support of the John Moriarty Foundation, they took part in several activities. On the occasion of this visit, Knijnik and Hunter spoke to the participants about how football can be a force for hope and liberation. I will come back to this meeting in a moment.

'This was the experience of a lifetime, but it won't be the last'

In the early 1960s, Freire travelled to the sugar cane fields of northeastern Brazil. He was trying to fight illiteracy in working-class communities. There he realised that only when people find the words and concepts to describe their situation can they be free. However, when Freire speaks of the oppressed, he does not only refer to poor social classes. He is also referencing those whose imagination has been 'colonised'. People often lose their voice and forget their ideals. They forget how they truly wish to commune, dream, fall in love, appreciate the beauty and important things in life, play football. They think and behave as others dictate. They underestimate their worth.

The first step towards liberation is giving voice to the oppressed. This will radically change their distorted self-image. They will become aware of their problems, strengthen their critical thinking, and imagine alternatives. To overcome injustice and oppression, they must first name them and communicate the need for resistance. Moreover, they need to find the words to imagine and experience justice, solidarity, and freedom. Knowledge and wisdom is found within people, in their relationships with each other and in the situations they have experienced, Freire asserts.

After people find the appropriate words to describe their problems comes the next step. New words and concepts help them understand their role in their community and the wider society. Through sharing common challenges, they can plan for their future. This is the moment, Freire tells us, when the culture of silence and fear is broken, and hope emerges. Through critically prescient thinking, they imagine freedom, utopia, and a world of opportunity. A new future will emerge from the changes now occurring in conditions of oppression. Dialogue and interaction between people is not just a means but a destination. It gives them meaning and courage to co-create a new future.

Hope and courage are concepts interwoven through Moriarty's life and work as well. Aboriginal communities have inhabited the island of Australia for 60,000 years. For 200 of those, their communities suffered at the hands of white conquerors. On 13 February 2008, the then Prime Minister of Australia, Kevin Rudd, formally apologised for the oppression, specifically the 'Stolen Generations', suffered by Aboriginal communities. However, much more needs to be done to overcome deep-rooted inequalities and racism. Intolerance persists in the country, Knijnik and Hunter point out. However, sport has been a vehicle for many Aboriginal people to share their values and personal stories with the wider Australian community. Moriarty is one of them.

By the late 1950s, Moriarty was a well-known footballer in the country and this reputation brought him financial security and acceptance. An unusual situation for an Aboriginal man at the time, according to Knijnik and Hunter. Moriarty had the opportunity to travel extensively and broaden his horizons. However, he continued to face moments of oppression and racism, like, for example, having to obtain permission to travel beyond allowed locations from the South Australian Aboriginal Protection Authority.

Moriarty's experiences led him to create the John Moriarty Foundation's football programme. Through this programme, young Aboriginal girls and boys were allowed to dream of a life beyond their small communities. With this in mind, the foundation planned the trip to the 2014 World Cup in Brazil. Brazil is a great footballing country and a visit there was expected to inspire them greatly.

Knijnik and Hunter examine this journey through Freire's pedagogical approach. For the Aboriginal travellers, it was a unique experience. They participated, as spectators, in the Mexican wave in the stands. They trained with the Australian national team where they were cheered on by 3000 spectators. They met other Indigenous communities and played football with them. Through intercultural dialogue, they not only encountered different attitudes, institutions, arts, and opinions, but by representing their own culture they learned more about it.

Moriarty recalls that 'our kids were provided with uniforms, the JMF gear, and once they put that on it transformed them – they are part of a team, and that's special'. The uniforms they wore on their travels allowed them to feel like they represented their communities. This feeling strengthened their confidence and self-esteem bringing them closer to their roots. They also experienced other football philosophies. Speaking to Knijnik and Hunter about the dominant coaching philosophy in Australia, Elvis, Moriarty's coach, and partner, says it treats talented players like robots. It stifles their creativity and freedom to express themselves.

This is reminiscent of the way formal education in schools usually works. That is, treating the student as an 'empty vessel', as Freire writes, an object to be filled with information and knowledge. The conventional education routine is akin to the logic of depositing money; educators, like depositing money into a bank account, deposit fragments of information or knowledge into the minds of children, who are regarded as empty vessels or passive recipients. Children are then assessed based on their ability to replicate and memorise the deposited information, emphasising rote memorisation and regurgitation over critical thinking and creativity.

As per the insights of Donald MacKinnon, a renowned expert in the psychology of creativity, creativity is not a mere talent but a distinct way of functioning. It isn't tied to one's IQ, but, instead, it hinges on the ability to immerse oneself in a particular state of mind – a state akin to playfulness. MacKinnon underscores the significance of dwelling in the 'open mode' rather than the 'closed mode' to nurture one's creative faculties. The open mode exudes a sense of ease, contemplation, and a playfully curious spirit, whereas the closed mode fixates on practical tasks and repetitive routines. For the educational journey to cultivate creativity, it must cultivate specific conditions, including providing the time and space for unhindered play, nurturing confidence, and, intriguingly, weaving in humour. In essence, it should foster an environment where the perpetual urgency takes a backseat, and a more playful and creative atmosphere thrives.

Education is a deeply political process, as most things discussed in this book. The design of any given educational process privileges some attitudes and perceptions over others. The 'empty vessel' approach and the 'closed mode' deliberately shape citizens who do not think as critically and freely as they can. It trains citizens to become cogs in the machine of wealth production and personal misery, mindlessly consuming in their free time.

The educational approach taken in a football training session is not an exception. When Elvis criticises 'robotic' players he means that instead you should 'let people be themselves and get the best out of them'. This requires cultivating critical thinking. The coach needs to pose questions and problems to be solved and then invite players to solve them. Players should understand that the real emphasis is on passionate participation, collaboration, and mutual support, rather than a mere demonstration of knowledge. This shift in attitude could foster a 'habitus' of solidarity, where these behaviours are expected to occur automatically.

The standardised programmes promoted by many federations treat players as mechanical pawns, unable to decide for themselves on or off the pitch. This reminds us of Marx's critique, as we saw earlier, of worker alienation. Football, for Elvis, is not a sequence of mechanical repetitions until perfection is achieved. It is an opportunity for young people to engage in a series of games and challenges to empower their autonomy.

Applying Freire's views to football, there is no real growth if coaches do not respect and understand the mindset of their players. One of the coach's essential roles is to attentively listen and cultivate an environment where players feel safe to share and express themselves openly. Creating this space fosters not just development but also encourages a deeper connection both on and off the field. This is how players learn to respect and understand their teammates, referees, and opponents. A main goal for any training activity should be for the trainee and the trainer to be able to put themselves in each other's shoes.

Cultivating empathy forges relationships between players, their coach, the team staff, the fans, and the community. It creates more balanced people who can meaningfully enjoy the game and produce true art. Elvis's vision for the pedagogical process of football reflects Freire's view of education in general. The ultimate goal of education is the realisation and experience of freedom: 'freedom from something' and 'freedom to do something'. Resistance, creation, emancipation. Defence, build-up, offence.

A recurring theme throughout Knijnik and Hunter's conversations with the 2014 trip participants was hope. Not as an abstract sentiment, but as perception of the capacity for change. Through football, Elvis says, 'we're trying to broaden their horizons in any way that we can'. Moriarty emphasises that the foundation's programmes go beyond football. They include multi-level education (e.g. conversation skills, knowledge of good health and nutrition) to provide young kids with important life skills.

Moriarty is trying to illuminate paths for young people to 'see beyond their little community and have opportunities and develop opportunities similar to what I've had'. For children who participated in the Brazil trip, write Knijnik and Hunter, that sense of hope was a main take away. The relationships they built and experiences they had on and off the field provided them with words, meanings, and stimuli to understand the world more deeply and meaningfully. As one child said, 'this was the experience of a lifetime but it won't be the last'. These words express the need, desire, and determination of young people to chart their own paths.

'What we want to do is make sure, with our football', says Moriarty, 'that we show there are a lot of other elements in life that they have to overcome and there will be many challenges, of course, but at least they can see that there is a pathway there'. The role of coaches is to ask questions to the kids so that, through collective discussion, they can feel all the different perspectives and choices on and off the pitch. Moriarty, Elvis, Knijnik, and Hunter don't have a specific football programme to propose. However, inspired by Freire and their personal experiences, they illuminate a humanistic philosophy for football and beyond.

The pedagogy of courage understands the problems of the future and calls us to change our destiny instead of accepting oppression. It cultivates passion and creativity so that together we can strive for a future that seems elusive. Even if we never grasp it. In the process, we will have taken a step closer to what each and every one of us truly wishes to become. Football can provide the space to rehearse our path to the elusive. To understand that this path can only be navigated through collective work and cooperation. 'I exist because we exist' as the African Ubuntu philosophy advocates, not 'you exist because I exist' as Michael Jordan might have said. 'When I hold a lantern for you, I am also lighting my own way', according to Buddhist philosophy.

This sense of togetherness should be felt by those involved in the art of football. Coaches, clubs, and federations must therefore look beyond the 'objective' and quantified criteria of formal training programmes. Beyond numbers and statistics. They ought to build into their programmes genuine acceptance, critical dialogue, solidarity, and honesty.

We all need to remember why we first played football. To seek that feeling again and again. To reflect on what we ultimately remember from the games we played and watched. The percentages? The leading scorers? The shiny shoes and gel-crusted hair of the players? Or do we remember an emotion that was valuable to us because we shared it with other people? Because we experienced it together?

My purpose with this book is not to present a new training and management programme for football, as I am not qualified to do so. However, established training practices could be enriched with a more collaborative, solidary, and creative spirit. To illustrate this, I offer an example from my research group's academic work in education.

Many of us recall the childhood game of musical chairs. As melodies filled the air, we would circle the seats – some of us prancing with unbridled enthusiasm, others cautiously eyeing potential resting places. When the music abruptly ceased, a frenzied dash ensued as children vied for the nearest vacant chair. Inevitably, one unlucky soul would find themselves without refuge, or two youngsters would engage in a comical battle of bottoms for the same perch.

Alekos Pantazis, now an Assistant Professor at the University of Thessaly's Department of Early Childhood Education, was pursuing his doctorate alongside me when he ingeniously adapted this time-honoured game. His goal was to elucidate the principles and practices of the commons to a broader audience. This reimagined version of musical chairs unfolds in at least two distinct phases. The first mirrors the traditional game as described above. Following each round, a thoughtful discussion ensues, encouraging participants to critically examine the implications of excluding group members. In the second phase, the procedure is repeated with a transformative twist: no participant is eliminated when the music halts. Instead, players are urged to collaborate, think innovatively, and share the available chairs, transmuting them into a communal resource – a true commons. Once again, post-round discussions focus on the participants' experiences of cooperation and shared stewardship.

Now, envision how such a game might translate for young footballers, with a ball at their feet. Picture a training exercise where, after each phase, players engage in reflective dialogue. These discussions could transcend mere tactical improvements, delving into shared experiences and fostering empathy among teammates. Furthermore, imagine scenarios where challenges demand collective problem-solving, mirroring the evolution of the musical chairs game. Rather than exclusion, players would collaborate, strategise, and share resources – the ball, the field space – as collective assets.

The transformative potential extends far beyond the pitch. Football, as a microcosm of society, offers fertile ground to nurture critical thinking about broader social issues. Coaches could catalyse discussions on fairness, inclusion, and respect, equipping players to navigate the intricacies of the world beyond the game. I aspire to future collaborations with coaches, managers, and pedagogues to collectively craft a more holistic training and management programme, particularly for developmental football – one that not only hones skills but also cultivates mindful, socially conscious athletes.

However, at the current critical juncture, the first step is to demonstrate a path for a new football in a potentially new world. This new world will not emerge on its own; it requires effort both on and off the pitch. So those who shape the art of football may realise that the fight for a more democratic and just world is the only fight worth pursuing to the end.

23
So how do we change the world through football

Our lives are affected by circumstances beyond our control. The colour of our skin, our gender, our potential disabilities, and the economic class we belong to determine our lives before we do. They place us at different starting points with more or no privileges.

The powerful of this world tells us: 'Run, win, excel and if you don't succeed try harder next time. Success is waiting around the corner for those who persevere'. But some of us, no matter how hard we try, will not succeed. 'It's your fault for not believing in yourself hard enough!' Life Coaches will teach us how to believe in ourselves so much that the universe will conspire to help us succeed. What if we fail anyway? Can we all succeed at the same time, or does one's success rely on another's failure? And what exactly is 'success'?

Every person's starting point is different. This creates inequalities and oppression. Through which elites emerge: the (over)privileged who fear losing their privilege. They do everything in their power to convince us that we live in the best world possible. That history has ended. They invite us not to dream: 'You naive children. These utopias of yours have cost us dearly. You're wasting your time – wasting our precious time too. There is no better than this world'.

If we believe that it is not naive to ask for a better world, then we are told that it is futile. That we won't make it. Because if we try, they will resist. 'You need us because we, the elite, produce your wealth. We give you work. We give meaning to your empty lives. We, the untiring creators. We, the ruthless geniuses dance and change trickle down. That's enough for you! Go back to your jobs. Workers produce, and footballers kick. Enough of your childish dreams!'

These elites, terrified of losing their kingdom, create institutions and structures that maintain inequalities. Their kingdom is like a Jenga tower. They will only allow a block of inequality to be removed if they are confident that their tower will not collapse and will continue to grow. These elites influence the way we produce, tax, discuss, dream, raise our children, flirt, and fall in love. They tell us what we should and should not do. What counts as success and what does not?

This, of course, affects the way we play and watch football. What is considered good and important? What is meaningful in the game, in the league, and in life? As we grow up in their world, we forget what we live for. We forget why we first played or first watched football. Or, worse, we never knew. We were born with a preordained mission. We play and watch football out of habit. We live by force of habit.

¡Ya basta!

It's time for a counterattack. For the big turn. To change the world with the ball requires defence, build-up, and offence; resistance, creation, emancipation.

We must resist all that divides us: racial, gender, class, and physical inequalities. Those involved in the art of football must stand for the oppressed. You might argue, 'but art is expression, important when honest and authentic, even if it doesn't take a stand'. Yet time is running out. We must take a stand at every opportunity, on and off the pitch.

After resistance comes creation. We must replace this rotting world with the one we envision. We need seeds that will quietly grow roots beneath the soil. And in the cracks of this stinking, crumbling world, and the new will bloom.

Envision a football where the scoreboard no longer displays the name of the scorer. Where the last touch of the ball before it crosses the line is not celebrated as an individual achievement, but as the culmination of collective effort. This small change could herald a profound shift in how we perceive and value football as well as every societal product. It would be a constant reminder that every goal (and product) is born from the sweat and strategy of the entire team – from the goalkeeper's distribution to the midfielder's vision, from the winger's sprint to the striker's finish. By removing the individual's name, we elevate the team's spirit. We recognise that in football, as in life, our greatest achievements are always collaborative. This nameless scoreboard becomes a symbol of our interconnectedness, a testament to the power of 'we' over 'I'. It whispers to us that the true beauty of the game lies not in individual glory, but in those who create art and a shared purpose.

A new world is already being created, founded on solidarity, cooperation, and sharing. In football, we can experience and anticipate moments of this new world we crave. Glimpses of a future that is being forged as I write these lines:

Oh yes, I see that day looming. The day when all we care about is that we danced together with a ball at our feet. For the story we write commemorates no cups or numbers. The story we write only commemorates those who strove for something greater.

For togetherness.

Sources and further reading

Chapter 1: Football is art
The ten-minute video discussion between Daniel Devlin and Socrates is available on Susak Press' Vimeo channel: vimeo.com/106209174.

Many titles discuss the nature and philosophy of football. One of the most prominent is Desmond Morris's *The Soccer Tribe* (2019, Rizzoli Universe). Morris suggests that our intense passion for football stems from our ancient hunting instincts. He argues that the act of scoring a goal is a symbolic re-enactment of the primal hunting drive, where the team become the hunters and the opposing team, the prey. This symbolic hunting, reflected in the competitive nature of the game, explains the worldwide fervour for sports, particularly among men. Morris contends that the entire process, from scoring goals to winning championships and celebrating with a feast, mirrors the ancient hunting experience, providing a deep and instinctual connection for millions of people. This is an opinion I don't fully embrace and the following chapters discuss why.

Another essential read is Stephen Mumford's *Football: The Philosophy Behind the Game* (2019, Polity). This book delves into the intellectual foundation that underpins football, leading readers through various pivotal issues at the core of the sport. While I largely align with Mumford's analysis in this book, my objective extends beyond merely comprehending football and its surrounding world; rather, I aspire to actively contribute to transforming both realms.

Chapter 2: The football gods are dead
Plato's *The Apology of Socrates* is available in free university libraries and wikis all over the internet. I thank those people who contribute hours to sharing knowledge freely.

Nietzsche's words are drawn from his book *The Gay Science* (1974, Vintage Publications). The book was first published in 1882 and a few years later, in 1887, Nietzsche enriched and republished it. *The Gay Science* is, according to Nietzsche, his most personal book. There he first formulated the view that 'God is dead'.

Chapter 3: We always dance together
This chapter is based on the article I co-authored with Alex Pazaitis, entitled 'Who Creates Value? Insights on Value Theory From *The Last Dance*', published in 2020 in the journal *Halduskultuur* (doi.org/10.32994/hk.v21i1.253). The words of the participants are transcribed from the documentary *The Last Dance*. Along with Alex, we created two short accessible videos on Value Theory, in Greek and English, which are freely available at: theotherschool.art.

Phil Jackson's book is titled *Sacred Hoops: Spiritual Lessons of a Hardwood Warrior* (1996, Hyperion) which he co-wrote it with Hugh Delehanty.

Chapter 4: We always sing together
Historian David Osinski's book *Worse than Slavery* (1997, Free Press) tells the story of the infamous Parchman Farm prison. He uses archival police and prison footage, oral testimony, and blues songs to document the horrors and struggles that defined Black lives in the deep American South over the past century.

The lyrics come from the song 'Early In The Mornin'. It is included in Alan Lomax's collection, *Prison Songs: Historical Recordings from Parchman Farm 1947–48. Volume One: Murderous Home* (The Alan Lomax Collection, Rounder Records). Sung by prisoners '22', Little Red, Tangle Eye, and Hard Hair. Their axes and pickaxes can be heard in the background as they work. At least as I write these lines, the song is free on YouTube under the title 'Prison Songs – Early In The Mornin''. Alan Lomax's words are taken from *Alan Lomax: Selected Writings, 1934–1997* (2005, Routledge).

Chapter 5: It came home

Coach Shields' statements can be found on the Guardian's YouTube channel under the title 'Northern Ireland manager Kenny Shiels: "Women are more emotional than men"'.

Data on women's unpaid labour can be found in the article 'The COVID-19 Pandemic Has Increased the Care Burden of Women and Families', by Kate Power, published in 2020 in the journal *Sustainability: Science, Practice and Policy*, which is freely available at: doi.org/10.1080/15487733.2020.1776561.

Chapter 6: So what is football anyway?

A growing number of studies, especially in the last decade, show the importance of cooperation in species evolution. For example, the study by biologist Roberto Cazzolla Gatti, published in 2016 in the journal *Biologia*, explains how ecosystems strive for cooperation rather than competition. The study is available at: doi.org/10.1515/biolog-2016-0032.

Also, several books have been published, in recent years, that present the not-so-well-known life of natural ecosystems to the general public. For example, one of the most iconic books is *The Hidden Life of Trees* by German forester Peter Wohlleben. Wohlleben explains how trees communicate with each other, have memory, and feel pain, presenting a new perspective on forest ecosystems.

Chapter 7: We all kicked a ball once

One of the hardest things in life is making sure a quote attributed to Einstein is actually Einstein's. On the internet anyone can write whatever they want and claim that an authority like Einstein said it, to make their point. The phrase I quote is from a book called *Living Philosophies* published in 1931 (Simon & Schuster) and includes quotes from 22 great thinkers, including Einstein. Whether or not it is Einstein who said the words in question (it probably is), it does not change the argument I am trying to make in the chapter.

Chapter 8: The one who always kicked the can

The Plague is one of Camus's best-known novels, in which he documents the lives of people in a world that seems without purpose or future. The meaning and purpose of life preoccupies Camus in most of his works, for example, in *The Rebel* and *The Myth of Sisyphus*. The latter two inspired me in the composition of the (extremely unsuccessful if the number of YouTube views is any indication) song 'Επαναστ-ηττημένος'. It's free on YouTube. Go have a listen, let's get that view-count up!

The Brothers Karamazov is Dostoevsky's last novel. It was published in serialised editions with the author dying four months after completing the work (1881). *The Brothers Karamazov* is one of Dostoevsky's most representative works. It is preoccupied with the concept of God, morality, and free will.

Chapter 9: The hallowed lost penalty

In March 2003, Susan Sontag gave a speech later featured in the anthology published after her death titled *At the Same Time: Essays and Speeches* (2007, Farrar, Straus, and Giroux). In her speech, Sontag pays tribute to the Israeli soldiers who disobeyed orders and refused to serve in occupied territories. Speaking of individual action and our collective fate as well as the relationship between morality, fear, and courage, Sontag says: 'Courage inspires communities: the courage of an example – for courage is as contagious as fear'.

Chapter 10: Messi stretches to infinity

A good introduction to the absurdity of growth, measured in terms of Gross Domestic Product, is the book by Giorgos Kallis, *Limits: Why Malthus Was Wrong and Why Environmentalists Should Care* (2019, Stanford University Press). Moreover, the report 'Decoupling Debunked – Evidence and Arguments Against Green Growth as a Sole Strategy for Sustainability' (2019, European Environmental Bureau) underscores the challenges associated with alleged green technologies, stressing the importance of re-evaluating green growth policies. It thus advocates for a shift towards combining efficiency with sufficiency as a necessary complement.

The former Brazilian president, Jair Bolsonaro, may not have explicitly uttered these words, but during his presidency, the deforestation of the Amazon rainforest reached alarming levels. According to Brazil's National Institute for Space Research (INPE), the forest lost an area between 1 August 2018 and 31 July 2021 larger than the landmass of Belgium. Vox Media published an article that succinctly outlines the impact of the Bolsonaro presidency on the Amazon rainforest. The article is freely accessible online under the title 'Earth's Future Depends on the Amazon. This Month, It's Up for a Vote'.

Chapter 11: The tragedy of our times

Upton Sinclair's famous quote comes from his book *I, Candidate for Governor* (1994, University of California Press). The book, first published in 1934, poignantly describes Sinclair's campaign that almost made him governor of California. It depicts the power games, conflicts, and control of the media by the economic and political elite.

Naomi Klein's words are from her book *This Changes Everything: Capitalism vs. The Climate* (2015, Simon & Schuster)

Chapter 12: When you're 4-0 down in the 89th minute, can you turn the tide?

David Goldblatt's statements were made in a Sky Sports report entitled 'Football's Toughest Opponent: Climate Crisis and the Fight for a More Sustainable Game' on 9 October 2022.

Data on the greenhouse gas emissions of the world's billionaires come from a study by Oxfam. US news network CNBC published an article on 8 November 2022, entitled 'Billionaires Emit a Million Times More Greenhouse Gases than the Average Person: Oxfam', summarising the findings of the study. The CNBC article and the Oxfam study are freely available online.

My analysis of the negative impact of modern technologies is based on an article I wrote with Andreas Roos for the *Harvard*

Business Review. The article is titled 'New Technologies Won't Reduce Scarcity, but Here's Something That Might' and is freely accessible online.

The 2016 study on carbon offset projects, entitled 'How additional is the Clean Development Mechanism?', is from the Öko-Institut Institute for Applied Ecology and is freely available online. The remaining evidence on carbon offset projects (e.g. in Cambodia) is summarised in an article published in the investigative journalism network ProPublica, entitled 'An (Even More) Inconvenient Truth: Why Carbon Credits For Forest Preservation May Be Worse Than Nothing' and is freely accessible online.

Reports on the environmental impact of the World Cup in Qatar come from two articles. First, from the article 'The World Cup in Qatar Is a Climate Catastrophe' published on 23 November 2022 in *Scientific American*. Second, the article 'Qatar's "Carbon-Neutral" World Cup Raises Doubts from Climate Experts', published on 7 November 2022, on the American PBS news network. Both are freely available online.

Chapter 13: The poor are poor because they make poor choices

Similarly to Chapter 3 in Part I, this one is based on our article 'Who Creates Value? Insights on Value Theory From *The Last Dance*' published in 2020 in the journal *Halduskultuur*.

Chapter 14: The tunnel to the other side of the earth

The argument I develop here for the depoliticisation of the economy and then to explain the impoverishment of African countries and the Global South in general is based on the book by the Norwegian economist Erik Reinert, *How Rich Countries Got Rich ... and Why Poor Countries Stay Poor* (2008, Public Affairs). Erik and I created a video that summarises the essence of his book. The video is available for free at: theotherschool.art.

A valuable source for the growing economic gap between the South and the North is the recent report (16 January 2023) of the non-profit organisation Oxfam titled 'Survival of the Richest'. For the football-related gap, I based the article 'World Cup Squads

Betray Divide Between Haves and Have-Nots' published on the international website of Deutsche Welle on 25 November 2022. The article is freely accessible online.

For the Zapatistas and other movements in South America, an excellent source is Leonidas Oikonomakis's book *Political Strategies and Social Movements in Latin America: The Zapatistas and Bolivian Cocaleros* (2018, Palgrave Macmillan). Subcomandante Marcos's letter to Galeano is freely accessible, in Spanish, on the website: palabra.ezln.org.mx/comunicados/1996/1996_07_08.htm. From there, I translated the content into English.

Chapter 15: The Cruyff turn
Dale Miller's patent can be accessed at patents.google.com under patent number US5616089A.

The text on patents, drugs, and vaccines is based on a three-minute video we created in collaboration with Els Torreele, a world-renowned researcher and advocate for social justice and health rights. The video is available for free at: theotherschool.art.

A landmark book in the debate against strict intellectual property regimes is *Against Intellectual Monopoly* by Boldrin and Levine (2010, Cambridge University Press). Baldrin and Levine summarise the arguments in favour of strict intellectual property and then deconstruct them using empirical evidence.

Chapter 16: So can the world change through football?
Le Guin's 2014 speech at the US National Book Foundation is available for free (text and video) on the official website dedicated to her work: ursulakleguin.com/nbf-medal.

Chapter 17: The turn of the century
The inspiration for this chapter was a song I wrote with Yannis Karakatsanidis called 'Τιατί η ιστορία δεν τέλειωσε ποτέ' (Why history never ended). It's free on YouTube where no more than 10, maybe 20, people have seen it.

I sourced information about Rosa Parks from the relevant entry on Wikipedia.

Chapter 18: Drivers should drive and footballers should kick the ball

I sourced information about Taylor, Vettel, Hamilton, Wolff, and Flick from the international English-language media. There was extensive coverage of all relevant events.

Amnesty International's report on the events surrounding the Qatar World Cup is freely available on the organisation's website: amnesty.org/en.

I have not been able to find the original source where Ayrton Senna spoke the words attributed to him here. However, as in Einstein's case in a previous chapter, the essence does not change.

Chapter 19: Democracy in football, democracy in society

The *Football Rebels* documentary series produced by *Al Jazeera* has a 25-minute episode dedicated to the Corinthian Republic (produced in 2013), in which many of the protagonists speak. Also in 2021, *Al Jazeera* released a 26-minute documentary on St Pauli titled *The Fans Who Make Football: FC St. Pauli*. Moreover, Carles Vinas and Natxo Parra's *St. Pauli: Another Football is Possible* (2020, Pluto Press) provides a rich account of St Pauli, politics, and football.

Regarding the commercialisation of football and its impact on fandom, Anthony King's works, *The End of the Terraces* (2002, Leicester University Press) and *Football in the New Europe* (2003, Routledge), provide a comprehensive analysis. These explore the evolution of football, particularly since the late twentieth century, scrutinising the prevalence of the free market, the emerging business class, and their repercussions on both the fanbase and the game itself.

On self-organised football clubs and their political action, you can read the article by Yannis Zaimakis entitled 'Reclaiming the Football Commons: Self-Organised Antifa Sport Clubs Against Modern Football in Crisis-Stricken Greece' published in 2022 in the journal *Soccer & Society*. The article can be found at: doi.org/10.1080/14660970.2022.2106975.

Chapter 20: Perhaps the greatest match of all time

The greatest match of all time was first shown in the second episode of *Monty Python's Fliegender Zirkus*, broadcast on 18 December 1972. Since then, Monty Python has featured it in various live performances (available on DVD and online) such as *Monty Python Live at the Hollywood Bowl* (1982) and *Monty Python Live (Mostly)* (2014). Terry Jones's statements are from a 2009 *New York Times* piece titled 'On Comedy's Flying Trapeze'.

Even though I have read most of Marx's published writings and books, the *Economic and Philosophic Manuscripts of 1844*, an unfinished work, holds the greatest fascination for me. The *Manuscripts* reflect the thinking of the young Marx at the time he was living in Paris, then the epicentre of socialist intellectualism. They include, for the first time, the foundations of his thought in what I believe to be its truest and most human form. It is from this work that my references to Marx's ideas come.

Chapter 21: Another world is here

Hardin's widely read and cited article titled 'The Tragedy of the Commons' was published in December 1968 in the journal *Science*. Ostrom's seminal book, in which she showed that another way of organising society beyond the state and the market is possible, is titled *Governing the Commons* (1990, Cambridge University Press). Also, in 2014, Paschalis Arvanitidis and Fotini Nasioka published (in Greek) the article 'Το Τσελιγκάτο: Ένας Θεσμός Επιτυχούς Αυτοδιαχείρισης Των Κοινών' (The Cheligato: An Institution of Successful Self-Governance of the Commons) in the journal *Το Βήμα Των Κοινωνικών Επιστημών*.

For peer production in the digital realm, I recommend that the curious reader explore the openly accessible article titled 'Are the Most Influential Websites Peer-Produced or Price-Incentivized? Organizing Value in the Digital Economy', published in the *Organization* journal (doi.org/10.1177/13505084211020192). Additionally, I co-authored an essay with my *Doktorvater* Wolfgang Drechsler on William Morris and commons-based peer production. The essay, titled 'Utopia Now' is freely available on the online magazine *Aeon*. This essay, along with all references in this chapter to William Morris, is sourced from his book *News from Nowhere* (2018, Martino Fine Books).

It is important to note some of the contradictions and problems faced by peer-to-peer projects mentioned in this chapter. On the one hand, modern technologies play a pivotal role in supporting and expanding peer relationships and the commons. On the other hand, technologies such as computers consume large amounts of energy in their production, use, and recycling. Also, workers, many of them children, work in deplorable conditions to get technological tools to the richest parts of the world at affordable prices. While the new technology commons is based on cutting-edge technologies, it appears to have the potential to radically change the way they are designed, manufactured, distributed, and used. Moreover, in recent years, in the absence of government support, more and more free/open-source software projects have been funded by large for-profit companies. The openly accessible article titled 'Beyond Global versus Local', published in the *Sustainability Science* journal (doi.org/10.1007/s11625-023-01378-1), delves into the ecological aspects of the peer-to-peer projects discussed in this chapter.

Chapter 22: The football of change

I sourced information about Paolo Freire's life from the relevant article on Wikipedia. The book I am referring to is published in English under the title *Pedagogy of the Oppressed* (2017, Penguin Modern Classics). There is also a collective volume on Freire's work entitled *Pedagogy of Solidarity* (2014, Routledge).

The article by Knijnik and Hunter, entitled 'The Pedagogy of Courage: Critical Aboriginal Football Education in Australia's Northern Territory', was published in 2019 in the journal *Critical Studies in Education*. It is freely accessible at: doi.org/10.1080/17508487.2020.1779768. It also includes a summary of Freire's pedagogy.

Donald W. MacKinnon was an American psychologist and professor known for researching the psychology of creativity. His book *In Search of Human Effectiveness: Identifying and Developing Creativity* (1978, Creative Education Foundation) presents an insightful examination of the core aspects of creativity and strategies for nurturing it.

In sociology, 'habitus' refers to how people perceive and interact with the social environment they are a part of, shaped by their personal habits, abilities, and character disposition. Pierre Bourdieu incorporated the notion of habitus as a fundamental element in his sociological framework, aiming to tackle the complex interplay between agency and structure. According to Bourdieu, the habitus is influenced by one's structural position and, in turn, influences actions. Consequently, when individuals engage in actions and demonstrate agency, they are concurrently reflecting and perpetuating the existing social structure. Michael Grenfell's *Pierre Bourdieu: Key Concepts* (2012, Routledge) provides a nice summary of Pierre Bourdieu's work.

The article titled 'Teaching Commons through the Game of Musical Chairs', authored by Alekos Pantazis, and published in the *tripleC* journal (doi.org/10.31269/triplec.v18i2.1175), provides a detailed exploration of how the musical chairs game has been ingeniously utilised to convey the principles and praxis of the commons.

Index

Aboriginal people
   cultural representation, 105–6
   football programs for, 102–6
   international experiences, 106
   John Moriarty Foundation, 102–6
   Moriarty and, 102–3
   resistance and rights, 102, 105
   Stolen Generation, 102
   youth development, 105–6
activism
   in football, 76–8, 79–84
   environmental, 76–8
   Formula One drivers, 76–8
   LGBTQ+ rights, 77
   political expression, 76–8
   racial justice, 76–7
   Socrates and, 79–84
   sports federations opposition to, 76–8
Africa
   football development, 59
   football talent drain from, 58–60
   minerals and resources, 56–8
   player migration, 59
   stadium attendance, 59
Akindes, Gerard, 59
alienation
   of footballers, 108
   of workers, 108
   Marx on, 88–9
Amazon rainforest, 41–2
   Bolsonaro and, 42
   deforestation, 42
art
   collective creation of, 20–3
   folk music as, 20–3
   football as, 7–10
   freedom of expression in, 37–40
   political purpose of, 37–40
   resistance through, 37–40
   social function of, 31–3
automation
   environmental impact, 47–51
   in production, 88
   technological solutions, 47–51

beauty
   in football, 8–9, 32–3
   Socrates (philosopher) on, 8–9
Beckenbauer, Franz, 85–7
Brazil
   Corinthians (football club), 79–84
   democracy movement, 79–84
   dictatorship, 79–80
   education in, 102–6
   Freire's work in, 102–6
   Indigenous peoples, 60–2
   labor movement, 81

Camus, Albert
   absurdity and meaning, 34–6
   football and philosophy, 34–6
   goalkeeper career, 34
   on revolution, 35
capitalism
   alternatives to, 92–101
   commons vs, 92–101
   critiques of, 44–6
   football under, 44–6, 79–84
   growth imperative, 41–3
   Marx's analysis, 87–91
   resistance to, 60–2

INDEX

Chicago Bulls
  collective achievement, 14–19
  Jordan and, 14–19
  Krause and, 15–16
  management conflict, 14–16
  Pippen and, 52–5
children
  Aboriginal programs, 105–6
  education through football, 102–12
  labor exploitation, 56–8
climate crisis
  carbon offsets, 48–51
  Copenhagen example, 48–9
  football's impact on, 47–51
  Qatar World Cup and, 47–51
  stadium threats, 47
  technological solutions, 47–51
commons
  definition and examples, 92–4
  digital commons, 97–101
  football clubs as, 83–4
  knowledge as, 64–6
  local management, 93
  open source software, 97
  peer production, 97–101
  vs privatization, 92–4
competition
  cooperation vs, 27–8
  in capitalism, 44–6
  in education, 106–8
  in nature, 27–8
cooperation
  in ecosystems, 27–8
  in football, 27–8
  peer-to-peer, 94
  vs competition, 27–8
Corinthians (football club)
  championships, 81
  democracy movement, 79–84
  political activism, 81–2
  Republic experiment, 79–84
  Socrates and, 79–84
  voting system, 80–1

democracy
  in football clubs, 79–84
  participatory forms, 93–4
  workplace, 79–84
Democratic Republic of Congo (DRC)
  mineral extraction, 59
  resource exploitation, 56–8

education
  Aboriginal football programs, 105–6
  banking model critique, 106–7
  critical pedagogy, 102–12
  football as pedagogy, 102–12
  Freire's approach, 102–12
  musical chairs example, 111–12
Einstein, Albert, 32
environment
  carbon offsets, 48–51
  climate crisis, 47–51
  football's impact, 47–51
  greenwashing, 47–51
  stadium sustainability, 47
equality
  Aboriginal rights, 102–6
  gender equality, 24–6, 77
  racial equality, 73–5
  through football, 102–12

FIA (Fédération Internationale de l'Automobile)
  political expression ban, 76
  resistance to, 76–8
FIFA (Fédération Internationale de Football Association)
  political neutrality stance, 76–8
  Qatar World Cup, 47–51
  women's football and, 26
folk music
  collective creation, 20–3
  Lomax and, 20–2
  prison songs, 20–2

football
  as art, 7–10
  collective nature of, 17–19
  commercialization of, 83–4
  democratization of, 79–84
  educational potential, 102–12
  political nature of, 76–8
  social change through, 113–15
  women's, 24–6
Formula One
  activism in, 76–8
  Brazil Grand Prix, 78
  Hamilton and Vettel, 76–8
  political expression in, 76–8
Freire, Paulo
  banking model critique, 106–7
  critical pedagogy, 102–12
  early life, 102–3
  football education, 102–12
  pedagogy of hope, 109–10

Galeano, Eduardo, 61
gender
  equality in sports, 24–6
  football access, 24–6
  stereotypes in sport, 25
  women's football, 24–6
  women's unpaid work, 26
Germany
  philosophers' football match, 85–7
  St. Pauli FC, 83–4
Goldblatt, David, 47

'Hand of God' goal, 37–8
Hamilton, Lewis
  activism, 76–8
  LGBTQ+ rights, 77
  racial justice, 76–7
Hardin, Garrett, 92–3

Indigenous peoples
  Aboriginal football, 102–6
  land rights, 60–2
  Mexican uprising, 60–2
  Zapatistas, 60–2
inequality
  economic, 52–5
  in football, 58–60
  racial, 73–5
  technological, 47–51
Iran
  women's stadium access, 74–5

Jackson, Phil
  coaching philosophy, 16–17
  Lakota influence, 18–19
  leadership style, 16–17
Jordan, Michael, 14–19
  Bulls dynasty, 14–19
  management conflict, 14–16
  Pippen and, 52–3

Klein, Naomi, 46, 50
knowledge
  as commons, 64–6
  patents and ownership, 63–6
  sharing vs restriction, 64–6
Krause, Jerry, 15–16

labor
  child labor, 56–8
  prison labor, 20–2
  unpaid work, 26
  worker movements, 60–2
Lakota philosophy, 18–19
Le Guin, Ursula
  on capitalism, 68
  on imagination, 68–9
  utopian vision, 67–9
leisure
  commercialization of, 83–4
  meaning in, 31–3
Lomax, Alan, 20–2

MacKinnon, Donald, 107
Maradona, Diego, 37–8

INDEX

Marx, Karl
  alienation theory, 88–9
  football and, 86–91
  historical materialism, 88–9
  predictions, 87–8
  theory and critique, 87–91
  value creation, 87–91
meaning
  in art, 31–3
  in football, 31–3
  through resistance, 35
Messi, Lionel
  commercialization, 41–3
  Saudi Arabia promotion, 41
Mexico
  NAFTA impact, 60–1
  Zapatista uprising, 60–2
minerals
  child labor in mining, 56–8
  Congo exploitation, 56–8
  technological dependence on, 56–8
Monty Python
  International Philosophy match, 85–7
  Pythonesque humor, 85
Moriarty, John Kundereri
  Aboriginal advocacy, 102–6
  football career, 102
  foundation work, 102–6
Morris, William
  News from Nowhere, 94–6
  utopian vision, 94–6
musical chairs
  commons teaching through, 111–12
  pedagogical adaptation, 111–12

NAFTA (North American Free Trade Agreement), 60–1
nature
  cooperation in, 27–8
  ecological connections, 27–8
  trees communication, 27–8

Nietzsche, Friedrich, 12–13

oppression
  Aboriginal people, 102
  resistance to, 73–5
  through football, 74–5
  women in Iran, 74–5
Ostrom, Elinor, 93

Parks, Rosa
  bus boycott, 73–5
  civil rights movement, 73–5
patents
  critique of, 63–6
  knowledge commons vs, 63–6
  medicine and vaccines, 64–6
pedagogy
  Aboriginal football, 102–12
  critical approach, 102–12
  football training, 107–12
  Freire's method, 102–12
  games in teaching, 111–12
peer production
  commons-based, 97–101
  digital examples, 97
  technological potential, 97–101
philosophy
  Camus and football, 34–6
  International Philosophy match, 85–7
  Lakota worldview, 18–19
Picasso, Pablo, 37
Pippen, Scottie
  Bulls career, 52–5
  contract dispute, 52–5
  economic background, 53
  Jordan and, 52–3
prison
  labor songs, 20–2
  Parchman Farm, 20–2

Qatar World Cup
  climate impact, 47–51
  environmental claims, 47–51

greenwashing, 47–51
labor issues, 77

race
Aboriginal rights, 102–6
civil rights movement, 73–5
discrimination in sport, 76–7
Parks, Rosa, 73–5
Reinsdorf, Jerry, 15, 52
resistance
Aboriginal rights, 102–6
in football, 76–8, 79–84
Iranian women, 74–5
Parks, Rosa, 73–5
through art, 37–40
Zapatistas, 60–2

Salk, Jonas, 64
science
mystery and creativity, 32
patents impact on, 64–6
Senna, Ayrton, 78
social change
football's role in, 113–15
resistance and creation, 113–15
through art, 37–40
through sports, 76–8
Socrates (footballer)
activism, 79–84
art of football, 7–10
Corinthians and, 79–84
death, 83
democracy advocacy, 79–84
Italian period, 82
on beauty, 8–9
political development, 79
solidarity
in commons, 92–101
in football, 102–12
Lakota philosophy, 18–19
worker movements, 60–2
Sontag, Susan, 39
St. Pauli FC, 83–4

technology
environmental impact, 47–51
inequality and, 47–51
mineral dependence, 56–8
peer production, 97–101
trees
communication, 27–8
cooperation, 27–8

United States
civil rights movement, 73–5
prison system, 20–2
women's football pay, 26

value creation
collective nature, 17–19
in sports, 52–5
Marx's theory, 87–91
Vettel, Sebastian
activism, 76–8
environmental advocacy, 77
LGBTQ+ rights, 77
women's rights, 77

Wieghorst, Morten, 37
Wiesel, Elie, 38–9
Wikipedia, 97
women
football access, 24–6
gender equality, 24–6
Iranian stadium ban, 74–5
stereotypes in sport, 25
unpaid work, 26
work
alienation in, 88–9
child labor, 56–8
prison labor, 20–2
unpaid labor, 26

Zapatistas
football and, 61–2
NAFTA resistance, 60–2
uprising, 60–2